COMMUNITY ACTION

COMMUNITY ACTION

A HANDBOOK FOR CATHOLIC HIGH SCHOOLS

Norbert Brockman, S.M.

University of Dayton

and

Richard Sullivan, S.M.

Charlotte Catholic High School

FOR OUR PARENTS

CONTENTS

INTRODUCTION

It is a somewhat threatening experience to prepare a work of this type. One is constantly aware of its inadequacies, and one is faced with the frustrating fact that so little has been written on the subject that a pioneer effort must result in inevitable failure. At the same time, with the development of greater understanding of community relations and community action, there are a number of secondary schools undertaking programs of civic and social involvement. A body of experience has been quietly building up, but as yet it is not a shared experience, and this factor we hope to help mitigate through this study. It is also obvious that many schools and faculty members are interested in introducing their students to community action, but feel keenly their lack of expertise, and are concerned lest the youngsters be exploited, misdirected, or badly influenced by an experience which they themselves hardly know how to evaluate. While this work is not instant expertise, it can offer some simple guidelines on relating the school to its community, and on the social formation of students on a practical level.

Perhaps some of the points made here will seem patently obvious. Yet it is the obvious that often escapes notice, and we have judged it better to include these things. Two of these points deserve special mention at the start, and the reader will find them reiterated elsewhere. The first is that the citizen, as citizen, has an obligation to his community. The emphasis of the past has always been upon specific civic duties such as voting, paying taxes, and serving on juries as the logical means of discharging this obligation. The very fact that we can think of any discrete action as discharging a communitarian commitment is an indication of the level of our thinking. What is demanded in the present day is an understanding of the dynamics of community and a real participation in its life.

The second obvious factor is that the foundation for community involvement on the part of the high school is the best possible school operation. A quality instructional program is a *sine qua non* of community participation. A faculty member in any high school has several titles to community participation. Not only is he or she a citizen, a part of the community itself, but also a professional person who has undertaken a public charge in the name of the community — the intellectual and social formation of its developing members.

At this point, we want to point out clearly the particular motivation which has been the genesis of this book. Our focus throughout is that of the Catholic school system, although most of the practical applications are as meaningful to the public school situation as they are within a religious context. Nevertheless, our concern is that the Catholic secondary schools in the United States, now so deeply involved in a reappraisal of their public role, relate themselves to the communities which they serve and better prepare their students to live essentially communitarian lives.

Consequently, what is attempted here is a manual that will help the Catholic school establish and enrich its community relationships. Extensive guidelines for community study focus upon getting an insight into community resources and operations. A tentative methodology for doing a simple community study from a school viewpoint, and for working with a problem census from a student viewpoint is a key to the practical issues involved. This is coupled with a series of profiles of major resource organizations and community institutions, their structures, types of services and information available, and possible areas of cooperation.

The Action Programs that follow the guidelines are examples of specific programs that have been worked out, tested in practice, and drawn from the experiences of a number of schools around the country. Clearly, the programs could be expanded almost indefinitely, but the initiative of the individual teacher will indicate what type of program will fit into the particular situation of a given high school. We hope that any number of programs and experiments will spin off from the suggestions and experiences reported here. There are a number of case studies of school-community action programs that have been developed in different types of Catholic schools. They differ greatly from one another, just as the situations in which they operate differ. We feel that this is the best way of illustrating the type of work being done at present.

Care must be taken that community action programs of any kind be related to the total school as an institution. The personal interests of the faculty will naturally be reflected, but community relations cannot be a matter of individual prerogative. With ample room for individual initiative, the program still should not be the private preserve of a clique or of an individual. Total faculty support should be sought insofar as possible. The nature and extent of this support will depend upon interest, time, and various other factors. It is essential that there be regular means of communication so that the entire faculty is aware of what is being done, how, and why.

The general norm for programs is that they should be of educational and formative value, therefore. The school's role is primarily that of supervision of school and student participation, and evaluation, and not project direction. Social organizations outside the school are structured specifically for this purpose, and attempts to usurp this function will be resented as being out of place, as, indeed, they are. (A rare exception to this is given among the Action Programs.)

Some teachers need to learn the hard way that adult supervision is a necessity in working with teen-agers in community action projects. This begins with good planning, which students are seldom able to undertake by themselves. The best planning is done by experienced persons in the field of interest, such as agency representatives, working with the teachers themselves. Often highly competent agency personnel have a very limited view of the capabilities of high-school students. The most important aspect of supervision beyond the planning stage comes in evaluation. There should be at least some group guidance (and preferably interviews as well) to help the student evaluate his work, his contributions and failures, and to smooth over the inevitable frictions that develop in any interpersonal situations of this type.

The teacher can expect a great deal of cooperation from community agencies, but few practical suggestions on the place of students in their work. Particularly to be avoided are programs that want students for exploitive purposes, especially programs with a political orientation. This is not to say that controversial issues are to be avoided; the very idea of such an involvement program will probably be controversial in some quarters, at least at first. Handled in a professional manner, with clearcut goals, however, programs will often surprise teachers by how little controversy they generate. The key word here is "professional." This presumes planning, consistency of performance, good choice of participants, supervision, evaluation, and the ability of the institution to finish what it starts; in short, all the qualities that make for good internal school operation and teaching as well. It is our hope that this work will be an aid to the development of programs with just these characteristics.

At this point, we feel somewhat at a loss. We are keenly aware of the inadequacy of trying to thank those who shared their thoughts and experiences (sometimes traumatic!) with us. Acknowledgements will always appear to the reader only as a list of largely unrecognized names. Yet any author finds these simple lists stocked with remembrances of repeated generosity, astute criticism, and valuable insights. Sometimes we accepted these,

5

and at other times we reappraised our views and decided to stick with our original judgments. We do not ask, therefore, that these people defend in every respect what we have said here. At the same time, we appreciate their contributions and value their viewpoints.

Two persons have made most valuable contributions. Brother J. Peter Dowd, S.M., of St. James High School, Chester, Pennsylvania, developed much of the preliminary design of the work, contacted and consulted some thirty experts in the field, and spent an entire summer working on the first draft. Reverend Henry Hood, S.M., Head of Zeal of the New York Province of the Marianists, offered so many practical helps that they can hardly be listed.

Among those who gave of their time and critical abilities should be mentioned Sister Mary Alfonsine, O.S.F., Principal of Alvernia High School, Chicago; Sister Rose Angela, O.S.U., Principal of St. Ursula Academy High School, Cincinnati; Dr. Jeptha Carrell, Director of Community Research, Inc.; Mrs. Hilda Curran, former Assistant Director of the Supporting Committee on Preventive Effort; Brother John Jansen, S.M., Supervisor of Instruction of the Cincinnati Province of the Society of Mary; Mr. James Kunde, County Administrator, Jackson County, Missouri; Sister Vera Troski, O.P., Dominican Sisters of the Sick Poor; Mr. William Markell, Executive Director of Sloane House Y.M.C.A., Manhattan; Brother Kevin O'Reilly, S.M., of the Governing Board of the Council of Directors and Moderators of the National Federation of Sodalities; and Mrs. Roger Ruppert, founder of the Special Committee on Urban

Renewal and mainstay of many civic and religious groups.

The original draft from which this study came was much influenced, and partly written, by a group of our confreres to whom we are much indebted. We would like to extend recognition to Brothers Richard Csarny, S.M.; Robert Bolz, S.M.; Paul Ciborowski, S.M.; Gerald Becker, S.M.; Joseph Kray, S.M.; R. Timothy Stein, S.M.; Joseph McNeely, S.M.; George Zehnle, S.M.; Thomas Timko, S.M.; and Lawrence Gray, S.M., and Mr. Robert Schult.

Brother Victor Edmunds, S.M., of Purcell High School, Cincinnati, and Brother Hugh Bihl, S.M., Sodality Secretary of the Marianists' Cincinnati Province, collaborated on Program Fourteen. Brother John O'Connor, S.M., of Dublin, Ireland, largely developed the material in Program Nineteen. To all of these people we are most grateful, although we alone bear responsibility for the final work.

Finally, Mrs. Penn Timpone served as our patient secretary, and the religious community of Marianist Preparatory School, Beacon, New York, extended harbor, hospitality, and companionship while we drafted the final manuscript.

NORBERT BROCKMAN, S.M.

RICHARD SULLIVAN, S.M.

PART 1
THE CIVIC COMMUNITY

Chapter One
THE ROLE OF THE CATHOLIC SECONDARY SCHOOL

Without hearkening back to the antecedents of so much of today's attitudes and activity — the YCW, the thought of Cardinal Suhard, the years of *Integrity* magazine — there has clearly been a quickening in interest shown in the development of urban life in the past several years. To put it bluntly, the city as a problem is an "in" topic of the day. Such a disparate collection of periodicals as the *Saturday Review, America, Life,* and *Scientific American* have devoted special issues to the city during the past year. A number of dioceses have become aware of the special factors involved to the point of establishing diocesan offices of urban affairs. Perhaps the single event in religious circles, however, was the publication in the summer of 1965 of Dr. Harvey Cox' book, *The Secular City.* Cox seems to have reflected clearly many things that numbers of people had only "seen in a glass darkly." The response to Cox' notion of "holy secularity" as applied to urban life has been nothing short of astounding. What is particularly notable is that the response has been so strong from Catholics. Cox has remarked privately that it has far outstripped that from his fellow Protestants. Was it, perhaps, that we were looking, in some fashion, for just the type of rationale that Cox

provided in *The Secular City?* This seems at least par-
tially so, and without endorsing all of the theological
implications of the book, one can see that many Catholics
read it with a certain shock of recognition. We might
only wish that everyone who read Cox with such enthusiasm had followed up with a careful perusal of Vatican
II's masterful document, the *Pastoral Constitution on
the Church in the Modern World.* The irony has repeated itself here: the Protestant response to this Council
document seems stronger than the Catholic one. Cox
served the catalytic function of bringing many of us to
a realization of the practical implications of the theology
of the Incarnation. One of the hallmarks of the so-called
"new theology" has been its extension far beyond theological circles. As the rich meanings of the Incarnation
are being renewed for us today, we are brought to reas-
sess the agencies and institutions by which we have
worked our apostolate in this country. As our thinking
has emerged from the shadows of the dichotomy between
matter and spirit, the social dimensions of our thought
take on color and shape. In the felicitous expression of
Teilhard de Chardin, "In our hands the world and life
are placed like a host, ready to be charged with the divine
presence of Christ."

The School and the Urban Environment

It is hardly necessary to rehash here the challenges to
Catholic schools made over the past few years, some of
them pertinent and profitable and others small-minded
and unrealistic. In the search for relevance that seems to
be the watchword for so much Catholic reassessment, we

are going through an agonizing reappraisal of our school system. Be this as it may, unless we see the challenges as opportunities, we may find ourselves hopelessly unable to communicate the very truths to which we are so firmly committed. And where does the opportunity lie? It is before us in the developing sense of urban community that we confront at every turn. And the relevance of this arises from the renewed sense of Christian community which we are beginning to see must be the essential mark of every Catholic institution. Let us explore some of the practical aspects of these theoretical, yet very dynamic, concepts.

The point of this is summed up in a trenchant remark of the late Pope John XXIII in *Mater et Magistra*:

> Education to act in a Christian manner in economic and social matters will hardly succeed, in our opinion, unless those being educated play an active role in their own formation, and unless formal instruction is supplemented by activity undertaken for the sake of gaining experience (Par. 231).

Rarely is it seriously argued that social formation stops at the classroom door, but precious little has been done in the past to structure any type of supervised and evaluated experience for our students. What has been done has operated through clubs and religious groups to a great extent.

One of the obvious characteristics of the Catholic Church in America has been that she is an urban church. The rural Southwest and central Kentucky remain as quaint reminders today, enclaves that demonstrate a Catholic pattern that never developed. The social patterns of today's Church are urban, post-immigrant, highly institutionalized — in short, marked with all the signs of a complex, industrial, mobile society. As a consequence, the Church has always had an urban apostolate in America, but seldom has her leadership had the insight to view this as an approach to the total urban community. Our parishes and our schools, our major institutions, have all had the flavor of conserving institutions. We taught a theory of social conservation and instilled a spirituality of withdrawal. It is popular to call this the ghetto mentality. Perhaps it was; but it seems better to view it as a necessary step toward the communitarian involvement that we now notice emerging. As much as involvement is emphasized here, it is not done so as a form of reaction. We have no more right, in this instance, to criticize the patterns of the past than the butterfly has to criticize the cocoon. Sometimes, in exasperation, we want to endorse the remark of Dagwood Bumstead that "all children should be born at the age of twenty-one." If this is more amusing than real, we still recognize that the social patterns of the past are not necessarily those of the present. Childhood can be cruel, and adolescence is painful. We have had our period of growth, and we must be moving on toward a deepening maturity in all of our institutions. "What is past is prologue," Shakespeare has Antonio say in *The Tempest*. One sometimes gets the uneasy feeling that there are those among us who would want the continuation of the patterns of the past beyond the need for them, precisely because they recognize their present inadequacies. If one builds a reputation on criticizing the past, it must be disconcerting to see true reform taking place.

With that, it is not surprising that we *do* have some difficulty in visualizing our work in the context of the total urban community. The Catholic community alone demands so much of our energies. And nowhere is this truer than in regard to the Catholic school system. Without neglecting a clear duty to our families and their children, however, we must go out to the wider community around us. In fact, it is for the sake of our students that we must do this, and it is the argument of this book that the Catholic school is the best agency we have for the task.

To have the school, as school, establish a wider relationship with the social and civic community will demand of the staff a civic mentality that may not have been part of its thought patterns in the past. In short, it demands a kind of urbanity that may be new to many of us. Frankly, urbanity in its several aspects has never been one of our hallmarks. To say of a religious, particularly, that he or she was urbane was to call into question his fidelity to his calling and to taint his spirituality. Spirittuality was not participation; it was withdrawal.

Today we must be urbane, or die. We are among the last of the great private institutions to be found in the urban community. In many cases our secondary schools, even when they no longer enroll students from the center city, are still found there. The reasons may be economic, but the fact is yet true. Every morning the Catholic secondary schools of the United States bring scores of thousands of teenagers from their suburban retreats into the hubs of the great cities of America. There is in this environment an opportunity for learning that the youngster in the suburban public school will probably never have. The tragedy is that every afternoon scores of thousands of Catholic boys and girls get on their buses and go back to the retreat of the suburbs without having been touched in any way by the urban dynamism all round them.

All the more curious is the situation of the suburban high school. We have all heard the teachers' stories of students who have been to far-away places on vacation, but have never penetrated the centers of the cities near which they live. That which gives cultural life to the place where they live is *terra incognita* to them. Those of us who have counseled college freshmen are regularly amazed by the remarks made by these young people to the effect that the campus is their first contact with "city life." It is not an uncommon remark from a student of a good, substantial, suburban family.

Perhaps it is too easily inferred that the flight to the suburbs has been a flight from relevance in too many cases. Be that as it may, here we are, and what can we do? The problems of the city are manifest all around us, and by ourselves we will hardly make a dent in them. Our obligation to try arises from many factors, not the least of which is our duty to be the institutions we profess to be; that is, educational and formational instruments for the common good. In a coordinated manner, therefore, working with other social and civic agenices, we can indeed affect the life of the city, and perhaps meet a few of its needs. Because our schools and school systems are highly institutionalized — a fact so often deplored and criticized — we can work realistically on the problems of urban society. *The paradox of metropolis is that only through highly institutionalized forms will the sense of community be reborn in the city.*

The opportunity is here. Too many administrators have reacted defensively to the criticisms of the younger generation in this regard, in the reaction of the "New Breed" against structured forms and agencies. We need to re-emphasize that structure is not the negation of the apostolate. If anything, it is its most valued means of meeting the needs of a highly organized society. It is a chimera to imagine that social problems can be solved purely on a one-to-one basis. Precisely because they are institutionalized problems, we must meet them with the answer of flexible institutions. The problem is not that we lack the means, but that we need some new understandings and some new techniques.

Where Do We Find Ourselves?

The first and basic understanding we need is the realization that schools are in a highly privileged position in American society. Few societies have accorded to education at all levels the support, financial and moral, that this country does today. Educational institutions enjoy great respect in American communities, and this has brought increased pressure for more and better education, usually in that order. The explosion of the community college movement is one of the elements in this expansion, but it has come at all levels. As a result, the school has become an agency of change as never before. It is the way up and the way out. Perhaps it is symptomatic of our response to the values of education that most of the programs of the War on Poverty are educational programs — retraining, head-start, upward bound, and so on, through a litany that constantly repeats our national conviction that education is the key to success and even to a sense of identity in this age of ours.

The second understanding that we need is that the urban environment itself is changing, and changing profoundly. In the relatively few years since the Second World War we have become an emphatically urban nation. Recent decisions of the Supreme Court make it clear that even the political balance of power has at last moved to the cities. What are the major changes and what do they mean to us?

An obvious and often-discussed social development has been the great move to the suburbs on the part of the middle class. The "flight of the white" has left a number of center cities divided curiously between the poor and the wealthy. Yet Catholic schools continue to serve a white, middle-class population, homogeneous in more than religion. And increasingly, our central schools draw their students from the suburbs beyond the cities in which they are located.

The major reasons that we have not followed many of our Catholic families to the suburbs are economic. We have heavy capital investments in real estate and buildings that cannot be lightly written off. Besides which, when a school system cannot have a secondary school in every neighborhood, it must consider transportation as a major factor in location. The simple fact in most cities is that public transportation does not adequately serve suburban areas. Often the center city is the only place where transportation converges to the extent that a central high school can serve a number of areas conveniently.

Certainly we are not the only institutions affected by these changes, and the effects have not been uniformly bad, as some seem to feel.

One of the significant developments among governments in the past twenty years has been planning. It is marked with one noticeable characteristic that we need to be aware of, however, and that is its regional character. Problems tend today to transcend artificial political barriers, and solutions can no longer be confined ones. The point in this for us should be obvious, but it is little appreciated in Catholic circles. The very fact that we have organized our schools on diocesan levels gives us a regional orientation. It is part of our thinking as well as of our day-to-day operation, and it gives us a flexibility that the smaller, localized, public schools may not achieve for many years.

The Practical Considerations

Now let us pass to the practical considerations that flow from the theoretical ones and from the situation outlined above. In orienting our schools to the civic context in which they find themselves we have too few concrete guidelines, and so this book presents several programs which are in effect now, and working well, as case studies of how some high schools have met this challenge. What characteristics can we isolate in the various programs that might present some guidlines and directions for expansion? To start with the obvious, supervision and control from the school is necessary. Even if immediate direction is in the hands of an outside agency, the school retains responsibility for any activity that it sponsors.

Secondly, the work itself must have an educational value. The primary concern of any school program is that it is formative for the student, and this calls for some type of evaluation. With the enthusiasm which a teenager brings to any kind of social involvement, it is quite possible for him to be carried away by the high adventure of the moment. Interviews and group discussion seem necessary so that youngsters can evaluate their own experience.

Third, community organizations themselves can and should provide much of this supervision. The real job of the high school is coordination and student direction, and only rarely project direction. Why should the Junior Catholic Interracial Council be under the direction of an overworked teacher when the local C.I.C. chapter could provide a competent moderator who would gladly work together with the school? The format that Junior Achievement has used successfully to teach students principles of business management can be applied to social and civic involvement. The difference is that in social programs, real and not artificial needs are being met.

At this point we come to the problem of expertise. If we would not think of appointing a faculty member as moderator of a school activity unless he or she knew something of the work involved, we cannot use teachers here on the basis of interest and enthusiasm alone. We will need knowledgeable personnel, successful in working with adolescents, aware of their limitations, and competent to criticize the programs offered the school to determine which of them will serve the ends of the total program. In the normal course of events, we should expect this competence from our lay teachers, whose proper concern this area of student formation should be. Nevertheless, the formation of our religious faculty and staff is of great importance, and some comments on this point would be in order here.

Forming Religious to a Civic Mentality

Much of what is said here applies, *mutatis mutandis,* to the formation of lay teachers as well. As far as the high school is concerned, however, it merely gets to pass judgment upon that education when the hiring process it going on.

While it is true that the formation of young people is infinitely easier than changing the attitudes of established staff members, we cannot write off our experienced teachers, as some would do in this regard. There are some real social aspects of our lives that we need to consider, and which contribute here and now to a certain social sense. One, obviously, is the communitarian nature of our lives. We need more conferences and discussions among ourselves to bring this central point more clearly into our collective and individual consciousness. Secondly, and as important, is the simple fact that religious get transferred! Our schools need to do less lamenting about personnel changes and more to capitalize on the advantages of a highly mobile personnel. Frankly, our experience has shown us that often the stable element on our faculties is the lay teachers. Given decent wages and tenure, they stay long after the religious they began

with have been moved on. Heretofore we have capital-
ized on religious stability, and now we must capitalize
on their flexibility. Religious can bring a wider range of
experience to even a cosmopolitan city school. It is truly
unfortunate that this urbanity of movement has left so
many untouched by the experience of having lived in
a number of civic communities.

The formation of the young religious, and in particular the ones in training, is the main point, however.
Programs of involvement are now much more common
than they were a few years ago, perhaps to the extent that
within a very few years they will become standard. The
program of the Jesuits in Chicago has been widely publicized, although one would think that a typical Jesuit
seminarian, considering his age and experience, should
be expected to have developed a great deal of responsibility for his own formation, and be capable of accomplishing useful work beyond his seminary studies. Far
more impressive are the activities of the postulants of
the Sisters of Notre Dame de Namur, who receive assignments as aides in public schools and various social projects during the period before they enter the canonical
year of novitiate.

Certainly one of the great benefits of such involvement
is the index given the superior of the student's response
to direction in a real situation. The experience should
be rotated and constantly evaluated by the young religious with his supervisor or superior. And because our
young people react so strongly to the false, the experience
must be meaningful. If the activities are "make-work"
the religious will see them for what they are — a contem-

porary form of watering sticks.

Many persons in formation today find themselves in the befuddling situation of trying to grapple with all the vague manifestations that are characteristic of what is called the "New Breed." Without getting into the various problem areas here, let it be said that supervised and evaluated apostolic involvement is one of the most meaningful tools of formation for this generation. With that bald assertion let's pass on to the final area.

What We Need to Do Next

In discussing what we need to do at the present time, one must begin with what is the central issue. Catholic schools are in a period of experimentation. What we need now is communication of what has been done so that programs in progress and those just beginning can profit from others' mistakes and successes. Within the Society of Mary, to which the authors belong, we have recently begun an organ of communication to detail the many projects being undertaken by our schools and by others. We need more of this on a national scale. Perhaps this might become one of the service projects of the Center for Applied Research in the Apostolate (CARA), recently established in Washington.

On a regional level, we need more urban affairs offices in dioceses. A large staff is less important than a central office for coordination and cooperation. In some cases, the local CYO office might provide this type of coordination for the high school, but usually it would not. We should at least explore the possibilities of other contexts. A further need to be served by such a central point of reference is the availability of information. Anyone who has dealt with the Chamber of Commerce in most large cities knows how much centralized information about a civic community can be simply assembled together, if only some agency does it. On the local level, contact with useful information is the greatest need. One hears this constantly in talking to inexperienced teachers in all types of situations. There is no reason why this need can't be met, and on a coordinated basis, for every school system. One possibility to be explored, especially for smaller cities, is a cooperative program with local church federation offices, which often have a professional staff in the area of community relations.

If a local information and coordination center would be valuable in every Catholic diocese, the same is true within the individual school and for every religious order. There should be competent resource personnel who can guide these programs, and the accent here is on *competence*. We have enough apostolic bloodhounds who will run down every trail that looks promising. What they seek, however, is adventurous activity, and what we need is something less individualistic. There are too many programs that fold up as soon as the one who established them leaves the school. We can never forget that the purpose of any program of student involvement in civic and social life must be geared to student formation and school service, and not be a flash in the pan.

One *caveat,* an important one, needs to be pointed out strongly in closing this chapter. While the focus of this work is on the involvement of the secondary school and its students in the life of the civic and social community, the authors do not intend in any way to deemphasize the academic life of the school. This is its unique role, and social formation of students is ancillary to this function. The school's mandate in the community is a formative one, and intellectual formation is a primary undertaking. Just as the Catholic secondary schools have learned that they cannot replace the parish, so they must see that they cannot become substitute social centers. The social formation of students will not succeed unless there is a good academic program to start with. Only a good school can develop community life in a real way.

The practical realization of this comes with the introduction of social participation into the school's program. As youngsters learn from these experiences, they will return to their classes more highly motivated, and seeking answers to many questions they hardly knew to exist before. What if they find their classes dull, repetitious, uninspired? Or worse, what if they are unprofessional, unprepared, lacking in direction and discipline? These questions need no answers for any professional teacher. Above all, students today insist upon integrity and honesty. Nothing will be more disillusioning for them than to find that the very moderators who are promoting civic and social participation are so absorbed in their outside activities that they do not do a competent job in the classroom. Consequently, the programs in this book are intended as suggestive (certainly not exhaustive!) of what may be done. Every school will have to assess its abilities and resources in order to decide what it can undertake. And this begins with a realistic understanding of the community which it serves.

Chapter Two
COMMUNITY AND MILIEU

The purpose of this section is to give an orientation to the concept of community, and to apply this to civic communities specifically. Before one can undertake any type of community action program or even begin to understand the meaning of one's own citizenship, there must be an appreciation of what goes into the communitarian relationship. It is not enough to proclaim "Solidarity forever!" as the socialists would have us do, nor even is it enough to invoke the basic rights of man. There must be realistic democratic life in an American community, and this must, in turn, be preceded by a grasp of the implications of this on the part of the citizens. The secondary school operates in this civic environment, serves a public purpose, and discharges the unique function of specialized preparation for responsible participation in the life of the community. It has, then, a unique obligation to know where it is going, and why it is headed there.

The Nature of Community

Every man belongs to several communities, and no normal man belongs to none. In the complex of social relationships that a man establishes, the interplay of community life looms large. It is in and through community that he takes on his own social uniqueness and personal position. His communitarian life determines his roles in life and much of the way that life is lived. Quite literally, it is in and through community that he finds his salvation. And this life he shares without losing his identity or individuality. In fact, he acquires his social identity through his communitarian life, and there is a real sense in which we can say that through community he most truly becomes a person.

Where there is a shared life and a shared good, one finds community. This is clearly apparent in the Church, the community of believers who live the shared life of God, who have an established relationship with one another (love, *caritas*), and who seek a God that is both immanent and transcendent, and is the cause and life of the community. Somewhat less obvious are the other communities in which man finds himself, beginning with the family, both the immediate one and the extended family of blood relationship, to communities of learning such as the school.

The civic community, which the classical philosophers have consistently insisted is a natural community, has its own shared life, which is political, and its own proper good, which we know as the common good. Problems arise when individuals and small groups live on the fringes of a community, participating in neither its benefits nor its decision-making. It is not unusual to find groups in society corrupted and depersonalized by this alienation. When this develops in a civic community, one can begin to isolate social problems which threaten the life of the community, because they begin to restrict its extension. When such a thing happens in an artificial community like the school, it is unfortunate, and the consequences may be wounding, but they can be overcome. A student who fails out of a university may suffer some disadvantages, but he can overcome them. But a citizen who must be driven from society is desperately sick; he either ends up in prison or in a mental hospital. The only hope for recovery comes when he is readmitted to the ranks of society; he cannot, like the poor student, rehabilitate himself outside the community which expelled him, simply because the civic community is a natural one. He has nowhere else to go; he belongs here in the most basic sense.

In any community we can distinguish four elements: it is organized, dynamic, real, and complex.

When it is said that a community is *organized* it is meant that it knows its own proper end, which is the good it seeks, and it is structured to secure it. The structure, in fact, is such an obvious element of organization that many people mistake it for the organization itself. While the goals must be shared by all, the direction of the community toward its ends is the particular function of authority. Authority is an essential service in every community, and again, many people find authority so obvious a characteristic that they mistake this role for the organization itself, and sometimes think of a total community as if it were only the authority which guides it. In short, a community is conscious of itself, shares a common goal, and is structured to pursue it.

To say that a community is *dynamic* is to add another essential feature to the notion of organization. There must be a life that the community shares together. The individual, in maturing and perfecting himself, does so most essentially by growth in prudence. It is this ability to take responsibility for free acts that enables the person to associate himself meaningfully with the good of the community and to recognize its counterfeits. By prudence the person becomes in reality what he must be — a free individual responsible for his acts, capable of sharing with others without exploiting or being exploited. He is able, in short, to establish a communitarian relationship with others rather than a selfish one. When free men associate for a common purpose this purpose becomes a shared good that transcends any one of them and yet is communicable to all of them. (The converse is not true. Shared evil does not produce community but the most radical individualism, because it turns the person in upon himself instead of out toward others.) The sharing aspect requires some sort of participation, which ordinarily is reflected in the organizational structure, and always in the symbolic ritual by which the underlying truths of the group are expressed.

Clearly, community life is *real*. To put it simply, it matters. If it did not, contemporary society would not concern itself so deeply with such concepts as "alienation," "belonging," and even that journalistic version called "togetherness." Every community makes a difference — a difference that counts — in the life of every one of its members. It molds his attitudes, protects his most significant interests, and helps to make him what he is. The decisions that matter are made by communities, and even those deeply personal decisions made by every individual in the course of his life are communitarian. If he marries, this is a public act; if he commits crime, the community punishes and seeks his repentance. The community takes very literally the remark of John Donne that "no man is an island, entire of itself." Aristotle's comment that the man who lives outside society is either a god or a beast has been intensified in Christian times: even the saint is expected to draw his inspiration from the Church. And society protects itself from the bestial man.

With all this, communities can be seen to be *complex*. For one thing, individuals belong to many groups, and share the dynamism of different ones. Sometimes tensions and even open disagreements arise among groups, and the individual must call upon all his reserves of prudence to choose the real good in a conflict, and not a counterfeit good. The individuals who themselves make up any community are persons of varied talents, interests, and degrees of dedication. All the characteristics that make up individuality are present in each one, and contribute to an immense variety of views, commitments, and values. And sometimes, of course, the values conflict with those of the community.

Organization of the Civic Community

The civic community is organized about five aspects: geographic, economic, political, social and demographic, and ethnic. These factors apply as well to a national state as to a local community, but in keeping with the focus of this work, the development here will be limited to a discussion of the local civic community.

The physical, *geographic* factor is often overlooked in attempting to study a given community. In reality, it is of great importance, since social problems tend to transcend artificial political barriers. Today in most parts of the country, regional arrangements of one type or another are being worked out in recognition of the fact that the space limits of a given city certainly do not contain the complete dimensions of the area, no more than they contain the total population.

In order to understand any community, one must begin with an overview of its land use. Business and residential patterns, segregated areas, ethnic ghettos, and the like are all parts of a total picture. Such policies as urban renewal and zoning will tell a great deal of what the future pattern of the city will be.

Beyond the center city lies the suburban area, either incorporated or not. Its relationship to the center city, whether it has industry as well as residential areas, the transportation available into and around the city, are major points about which to be informed.

The relation of the school to the community on a physical level may be slightly less clear. The administration will be keenly aware of factors that require special bus service, but there may be no clear idea of where the student body comes from. Some accrediting agencies ask that this information be assembled periodically, and if the information is recent, an interesting student project can be the drawing of an area map plotting student homes. The Catholic high school in particular should know the location of each of the parishes and elementary schools that it serves, and the type of transportation available to and from each neighborhood with a significant Catholic population.

Housing conditions themselves, although a consideration in zoning, lead into the *economic* factor. A neighborhood of large apartment buildings will have a different character than one of single-family dwellings. The location of many facilities, especially shopping and recreational centers results as much from economic considerations as spatial ones.

The most important economic questions for the school involve family employment and opportunities for student employment after graduation. When unemployment is high, business are relocating elsewhere, and a large percentage of students cannot go on to college, the usual pattern will be that many alumni of the high school will not stay in the city for very long after graduation. Few of the college graduates will return, and armed forces enlistments will be high. This is the pattern of a city in economic crisis. It may result from the failure of a major industry that dominated the town during a prosperous period. Job opportunities for minority-group members will often be a key to understanding social problems involving them.

The *political* life of the community is one of the first things a teacher thinks of in attempting to study an urban area. While it is usually less significant than suspected by many, it is never insignificant. Ultimately, all major problems are political in the broadest sense; that is, they are public issues calling for public solutions. Besides this, many of them become governmental issues. This is especially important in the developing area of federal-urban relations. With the establishment of the Department of Housing and Urban Development, federal programs can be expected to expand. Even at present, the federal government provides major funding for many social programs, including the Poverty Program, Social Security (through the states), public housing, and aid to public education. An important understanding for every citizen is that local federal offices constitute part of the local government structure, although not in the traditional way.

The structure of the local government and political parties can usually be discovered rather easily. The teacher is interested in knowing if there is a tradition of professionalism in government, or if he will be dealing with agency representatives whose primary loyalties are to political organizations that appointed them. He is also interested in finding out to what degree area governments cooperate on common problems, if they do at all. In getting information about suburban governments, their ability to provide basic services comparable to that of the center city is significant. The tax structures enter into this as well.

Social and demographic patterns are of most immediate concern to the secondary school. Not only should there be a grasp of the total patterns of the community, but also of the special patterns of the Catholic subcommunity which the school serves. Population distribution is quite significant, since younger families with numbers of children often tend to cluster in certain suburban areas, with resulting pressures on schools. The elderly may also cluster in older areas of a city. In addition, patterns of mobility are important in understanding the character of shifting populations and declining areas. The location of white-collar, blue-collar, and professional persons may be of interest. After determining the social classes of the area, the teacher will want to know how the school's student body reflects these patterns. He may find that he has a cross-section of the city's social classes, or that he is dealing with a special group. It is also important for the Catholic school to know if the Catholics of the community are themselves representative of the total population.

Even in this post-immigrant age, *ethnic* factors are important, perhaps especially to the Catholic school. If the city's churches include several national parishes, there may be unique contributions made by the various cultural groups. The relations of the Catholic community in general with other religious groups can tell the school much about intergroup relations. Often the Catholic high school, as a sort of central facility, is expected to show some leadership in ecumenical affairs, but the school cannot become involved until it knows the traditions of the Catholic community and the attitudes of the local clergy on the matter.

Relations between Negroes and whites are today of great importance in every city, but newspaper accounts of cooperation and tension can often be deceiving. It is easy to view the Negro community as if it were a middle-class group with middle-class values. Sometimes one will find that Negro leadership represents only a small but articulate group among Negro business and professional people, sometimes rejected and scorned by the bulk of Negroes.

The Community Decision-Making Process

It is always considerably easier to get factual information on the organization of the community than on its dynamics. The structure is always at the service, so to speak, of what makes it tick. Major decisions in the community may be made completely in the public forum, with full debate before the city council or some similar responsible group. Just as often, however, important decisions are made by people who are not responsible to the public, and who hold no public position at all. The decision-making process in any community is rather diffuse, involving public figures, significant groups, business concerns, political parties, and others. Part of the character of the community derives from the type of community leadership that has evolved.

At the turn of the century, the Swiss political scientist Roberto Michels coined the expression "the iron law of oligarchy" to describe the phenomenon that in all large groups a small elite always takes control of policy. Political scientists today, in applying this concept to communities, tend to speak of "power structures" and "elites" that control policy-making in every community. The first reaction of many observers is one of distaste. They instinctively reject the notion that a community should be governed by anyone other than "the people," or by any other means than free elections to choose representatives. On closer inspection, however, the idea of elites is less repugnant. A democratic system is at its most mature level when it involves a large number of the public in its activities. It is a natural development for leaders in various areas to become leaders in civic affairs, and there is no particular reason why all decisions in a community need to be made in a single forum. Of much greater importance is how responsive the power structure is to public needs, and how altruistic its motivation.

The first basic understanding here is that very few communities will have a single power structure. There may be a small, informal group of important men who do influence decisions of the broadest kind. Within particular subgroups, however, other influentials will be at the center of the policy-making process. Ordinarily the Negro community, if it is of any size at all, will have its own influentials, who will sometimes be political leaders, but will always include the most prominent ministers, and occasionally certain businessmen (funeral directors, for example). In many cities it would be difficult for a school action program involving the Negro community to be undertaken without at least tacit approval of the Negro leadership.

Where there are strong ethnic groups that have retained their cohesiveness, the elite may consist of the heads of the most respected families. Many an Italian community accords great respect to the *patrones* who lead its major families. While this paternal clan pattern is unusual outside national groups, it is of some significance to the Catholic school, since many ethnic groups in large cities are predominantly Catholic.

The leadership in various subcommunities, whether

social or economic, may also be regarded as part of the larger power structure of the entire city. Business leaders often, for instance, have influence in many fields outside of commerce. They may be concerned deeply about education and social welfare, sometimes because a stable community is important to their businesses and good schools significant for their recruitment of quality personnel, but often simply because they are committed to a better community.

In short, in any city there will be a pattern of multiple leadership, made up of influentials from different classes and strata of society, and with roots in varying subgroups.

The smaller high school should not regard all this as being tangential to its interests. Even a parochial high school that serves only a limited neighborhood should find these ideas meaningful. In many cities, there will be neighborhood councils or improvement groups comprised of respected residents of the neighborhood who are concerned with area development. It is often at this level that such controversial issues as integrated housing, recreational facilities for youth, and the like are confronted. Interestingly enough, the organization of many of the programs of the War on Poverty begins with neighborhood committees. Such groups can be influential on issues like zoning, urban renewal, and other neighborhood interests.

Neighborhood councils lead naturally into an important consideration: widened participation. The wider the participation in civic activities, the more mature the level of decision-making in the community. This simple rule-of-thumb can be very meaningful to the secondary school. If decision-making is broadly based, it is more likely that any type of problem can find an agency or group interested in its solution. In a well organized community, resources for dealing with problems are greater, and the school will find representative groups to which it can relate itself. It is also easier to find outlets for student activities in such a situation.

In a later section of this work a list of community resource organizations is given. To some extent, each of these deals with public policy. Some are of greater importance than others, and some have broader interests than others, but together they are the key to understanding how the community comes to know that it has a problem or becomes aware of a need, and how it meets its needs.

Community Problems

In any community, expected benefits for community members must be forthcoming if the community is to fulfill its function and preserve its existence. It must meet the expected needs of its citizens, produce what it is structured to produce, adapt to new situations, and develop new programs to meet needs that arise. The latter point includes something that in many cases presents difficulty: recognizing the existence of a new problem or need that has arisen, and which the community has not dealt with before. In recent years, for example, the need for expansion of higher education has become quite apparent, and many communities have been willing to tax themselves in order to provide community colleges. A few years ago not many communities were willing to recognize this need, and the pattern of community college development is often an interesting study of awakening public consciousness and mobilizing forces to provide new facilities, often at great cost.

In addition to providing for new needs, breakdowns in social structure need to be repaired. Sometimes social disorganization can go on for years without adequate response from the community, usually because the people more affected are not articulate or are poorly represented among the influentials. An example here are the elderly indigent. In some cases, a social problem may be so unpleasant to a given community that there exists a consensus to ignore the issue rather than damage the image of the community. This unhappy situation is not unusual in regard to juvenile delinquency in prosperous suburban communities. The essential problem in both these cases is one of community mobilization. In some manner the needs of the community must be articulated and brought to the attention of the influentials who, in turn, can organize community resources to deal with the issue. In a few cases this done dramatically, as by a newspaper exposé ("Teen-Age Brawl Raided by Police!"), or by an election upset caused by widespread dissent. More often, one hopes, civic groups will attempt to arouse public interest in the problem until support for various solutions is mustered. Although the solutions may be incomplete, they are usually at least a beginning.

A not uncommon example occurs when a women's club becomes aware of the problems of the elderly poor living in rooming houses in declining neighborhoods of a city. They may want to provide a Golden Age Center so that some congenial companionship is available, but they will soon discover that to do that may require support from public agencies, local foundations, and concerned business groups. The logical approach must begin by convincing various influentials that there *is* a problem which is being neglected. As the dimensions of the problem come to light, various other groups in the community may begin to participate. Volunteer associations will help provide assistance of different kinds; school groups may offer to present periodic entertainment. In several cities, for example, civic associations have begun a service of delivering meals to the homes of elderly persons who cannot easily go out to eat and who cannot cook for themselves. Gradually, what was the concern of a small group becomes a total program involving many groups and individuals, and even larger in scope than was originally conceived. A community and its resources have been mobilized around a need, and as more people and groups become involved, different aspects of the problem come to be met. The illustration used here may seem far from the immediate concerns of the high school, yet it is the type of program to which high-school students can easily contribute meaningfully.

The school is aware of some social problems because they affect the student body directly. If there is a high degree of family disorganization, lack of proper after-school recreational facilities, or high unemployment, one will hardly have to look very far to discover them. They will be obvious in everyday conditions. A school that must provide free lunches to a number of youngsters each day knows that it has a poverty problem. If a substantial number of Appalachian migrants enter the school with woefully inadequate academic backgrounds, every teacher is aware of the problem immediately.

Many school-centered problems are solved in Catholic high schools by eliminating the student, and therefore the problem. While Catholic high schools admittedly have limited resources, and usually cannot provide reading clinics, school psychologists, or school social workers, shifting problems to the public schools by an annual exodus of transfers seems hardly a reasonable alternative. In many cases, services such as school nurses, remedial help, and the like are available to Catholic schools from the public school system. Too many Catholic schools are reluctant even to keep students with academic problems, much less those with deeper-seated difficulties. This has, of course, enabled some Catholic secondary schools to maintain a high-status image in the community, usually on the basis of high acceptance rate into colleges. A school which has consciously chosen to serve such a group would seem to have taken on also the obligation to do something concrete about the social formation of these students, lest the school graduate an alumni of status-seeking, unchristian social climbers.

Chapter Three

GUIDELINES FOR COMMUNITY STUDY

Much has been said here of making ourselves and our students aware of the urban community, of involving the faculty and the students of our high schools in that community, and of emerging from the ghetto which has long isolated the Catholic community. This has been said in Catholic journals for the past ten years, but few have been bold enough to venture forth and tell us how we can do it. It is a rather frustrating experience to listen to sermonizing on the ills of a high school which trains its students in isolation from the realities of society around them and then to find, after the sermon is finished, that we have been provided with nothing but foam and froth with little to go on. To avoid some of this, this section has been composed to enable both faculty and students to learn about the urban community, to come to grips with the vague term "community," and to do this learning in an organized and formative manner, in such a way that the collecting and cataloging of materials will of itself be a learning experience.

There are a variety of ways to approach the actual process of making a study of a specific civic community, depending upon the depth to be attained, the perspective to be gained, and the actual use intended for the completed study. While it is true that involvement in the community will follow for a select few if attention is centered upon one particular problem — poverty, for example — an approach such as this tends to be very limited in scope and the formation given in such a program is far from what is possible. An approach which centers itself around one particular problem can be very fruitful, however, if some groundwork precedes it. No program or problem can adequately be considered in isolation. Preliminary work in the form of seeking out the basic institutions, activities, problems, and needs of the community will provide the necessary context for dealing with the issue and planning the program.

Often, this work may seem tedious, slow and rather bland. Yet it is the foundation upon which truly coordinated high school social formation programs are built.

The following points are suggested as appropriate steps and initial guidelines to be taken to obtain a broad but useful view of the urban community.

To begin with the obvious: the newspapers can serve another function aside from being used to wrap the garbage. An attentive reading of the city newspaper can give a general feel for the life and spirit of the community — community-wide interests, problems and issues, key personalities and socially prominent individuals, events within and around the community. Much important local news can be gathered concerning educational, religious, business, political and other organizations within the community. Also, this information can be found every day (keeping knowledge of the city up to date). This makes simpler the process of clipping and filing important items to be saved for future reference.

Aside from gathering such news material, it is important to follow the editorial positions and feature articles and series on institutions, people, and community-wide issues. Sometimes letters to the editor reveal community response and concern on various questions.

Neighborhood newspapers, or those serving particular groups (ethnic, religious, or economic) can provide an insight and a feel for the life of various subcommunities within the general urban community.

Through the use of detailed street maps and census tract maps it is possible to become familiar with the names and characteristics of various neighborhoods in a community. Size of a neighborhood, population density, the use of land in a neighborhood, and evident class and ethnic concentrations can be picked up from such maps. Two significant notions for understanding a neighborhood — housing conditions and land use for industrial and commercial purposes — come directly from a careful study of such maps. Census tract maps can also provide much information regarding the social layout of a community and demographic characteristics such as educational and occupational status of a given area. Many times they can indicate the key social problems of a certain neighborhood or area of the urban arena.

Of course, a complete understanding of a neighborhood can never be obtained through the use of studies, graphs, charts, surveys, files, resource books and the endless amount of reports available. To appreciate a neighborhood more is necessary than a statistical abstract. Too often teachers and students, having completed a survey of a particular area, will go forth to confront the area's problems with no real, concrete knowledge of the neighborhood. Aside from the obvious imperfection of attitude, the individuals in this case fail to see that personal contact with people in the neighborhood is irreplaceable. A real feeling for the pulse of a neighborhood comes through conversations with local residents, merchants, and leaders. This information cannot be obtained in any chart or table or any graph or report. This is perhaps the most important insight if one is going to understand and appreciate the urban community.

For high school students, a very useful way to break out of the statistical approach is to organize a "windshield survey" of a neighborhood. They simply drive through the area, trying to list major characteristics and notable landmarks. While superficial, this technique does begin to fix an image of the neighborhood, its life and color, on the students' minds. Accompanied by an area leader, they will begin to see with his eyes what the community is like. If effectively organized, this can prove a worthwhile experience for the students and help them make their learning more vivid and a bit more personal. Then, when a certain neighborhood is mentioned in the news, the student who has toured through the area with an experienced neighborhood leader will have a tendency to associate the ideas in a better manner.

Many high schools are required to conduct self-study surveys as part of the accreditation procedure of regional associations. The data obtained and the process by which much of this information is collected can prove invaluable for an initial introduction of the entire faculty to the realities involved in the school-community relation-ship. The regional associations usually require a state-ment regarding the school-community relationship as part of the self-study report.

The evaluative criteria for accreditation asks for stu-dent-related material such as geographical distribution of students among the areas from which the school draws, parish listings, drop-out ratios, occupational and educa-tional goals of seniors, and career choices of recent alumni. Accrediting teams also look for other related information: educational and recreational facilities in an area, an outline of the school's socio-economic classes, and the like. All of this information, as general statistics, is of continuing value to the teacher.

The use of newspapers, maps and self-study programs will provide much initial information concerning the civic community. However, unless an effort is made on a rather systematic basis to contact key organizations and agencies to obtain information in the form of studies, profiles, census data, and program studies of various city-wide problems, much of what is learned will remain sketchy. At the same time, contact with such resource organizations will suggest various types of projects which can be commonly worked out between the agency and the school. The process of contacting such groups and of working out a program lends itself to making the gen-eral urban community come alive in the minds of stu-dents. Agency heads are ordinarily quite willing to talk over their problems with teachers, and are usually open to sensible suggestions of cooperation between the agency and the school. Just as a neighborhood becomes real through personal contact, so institutions are made concrete through visitation. Organizations common to most urban areas will be listed and described in the next chapter.

Contact with major resource organizations will provide most of the information needed to come to an understanding of the urban community. Such agencies as the city and county planning boards, a public library, a League of Women Voters, and some type of community research organization are ideal in this respect. However, aside from those agencies which touch the entire community through the people they serve, the studies they issue, or the problems they are concerned with, there are a variety of important organizations serving specific groups of people. These groups produce studies and other types of information about their own structure and organization, the types of people they most frequently contact, and some of the community issues of particular importance to them. Such groups are church organizations, school boards, civil rights groups of various shades of opinion, and universities or local colleges. It is important to know them and what they know about the community.

If any kind of continuity is going to be maintained and if the work of one group is not going to be lost by the next, some type of library should be organized — possibly as a special section of the high school library — which would be concerned with community affairs. Such a library is invaluable for offering both the faculty and student body an opportunity to learn about the community through the acquisition of reports, profiles, and

studies of various organizations. A library enables a new
faculty member to become familiar with the city without
going through the entire process described here. Selected
readings of reports, studies, and profiles of various resource groups will bring him up to date in a relatively
quick fashion.

There are a number of ways to organize an efficient
and usable community library. It may contain information about local issues only, or include regional issues
as well. Files may be organized according to various
categories: communications media, educational, community service, political, religious institutions, general
population statistics, etc. This approach groups problems, statistics, and resource organizations together. For
example, the drop-out problem would be grouped with
the Board of Education under an education file. Another
common approach is to organize one file according to
institutions and another file according to problems and
projects. The advantage of the first system is that it con-
nects a problem immediately with the agency geared to
do something about it. The advantage of the second is
its ability to demonstrate quite vividly the interaction
of innumerable agencies upon a single problem. Obviously, a file dealing with poverty as a social problem
must include a description of the projects being carried
out by business, educational, religious, government, recreation, and neighborhood groups working on various
aspects of the question.

A file of important and useful clippings from the newspaper should be kept if the library is to be constantly up
to date. Agency heads, leaders of various civic groups,

even the orientations of many civic institutions themselves, change often enough to necessitate a running file with the most recent information. The filing of newspaper clippings serves this purpose well.

It is not necessary to clip every item having something to do with the civic arena. As experience develops, certain areas will take priority as the school centers itself in a particular direction. Initially, however, the file should be broad enough to cover the major institutions, personalities, problems, and projects in the city.

One of the most interesting and important things to learn in any given community is the manner in which various persons relate with other people in the influencing of trends and events. This knowledge becomes very valuable in tapping resource personnel for school programs and projects. Often, communication with persons in positions of importance in a community can prevent the school from blundering in either the choice of a project or the emphasis and direction of a particular project. The compilation of a file on leading personalities and resource persons in the community shows different levels of community involvement and influence that a particular person or group of persons possesses.

A community affairs library should have a section for bibliographies and publication lists from various national, regional, state and local organizations. Listings of professional groups, educational developments and programs are examples of the types of materials which could be incorporated into a community affairs library. Complimentary subscriptions to the publications (such things as newsletters, pamphlets, bulletins) of international, national, state and local organizations can give useful insight into trends, issues, ideas which are going to affect large numbers of people in the groups and agencies with which the school is going to come in contact.

A library such as this must be constantly kept relevant. Clippings referring to older events are valuable as background, yet what is more important is information concerning present conditions and situations. A school club, or a group from a social studies course could be formed to keep the library functioning as a tool for understanding the urban community. The obvious educational value of such a collection of materials hardly needs stressing.

Through the use of newspapers, maps, materials from major organizations, and personal contacts, a clear picture of the institutions, problems and processes of a civic community can be attained. It is also valuable to discover what the residents feel and think about their city. What does the community think of itself? What is its public image? The answers to these questions are valuable for a school — what do students, parents, alumni, and community leaders and residents think about their community, the school, its academic excellence and community service? Opinion surveys, although not as professionally done as Mr. Gallup's, can be conducted by the school, and if a few minimal safeguards be followed, can at least point out some generalizations of considerable value in school planning. Some examples of such surveys are given in the section on the Action Programs. Many schools speak of updating without any clear idea of what areas need a revitalization and what priorities should be set up to determine areas of development. Money spent on public relations is thus wasted, and the original intent is probably not achieved. Opinion surveys, while not the entire answer, can at least go far toward removing much of the guesswork which too often takes the place of planning on the basis of good information.

The above-mentioned areas were not meant to be steps in a series, as if contacts with resource organizations could not be made until both the newspaper had been thoroughly taken apart and the walls of the faculty lounge had been covered with maps of all sizes and shapes. Rather, this is meant to highlight certain tools which can be used to unlock the secrets of a large metropolitan community. The use of newspapers, maps, resource organizations, making personal contacts, conducting a self-study program and an opinion survey, obtaining subscriptions to publications of various groups — all were described here even though many teachers will find them obvious. Yet, how many Catholic high schools have gathered even these simple resources? Mundane though the activities described here may be, they are a marvelous corrective for theorizing in a vacuum. If apostolic programs and possibilities beyond the four walls of the school are going to take place in a concrete and realistic fashion, those organizing and directing them must have competence in understanding the city and its subcommunities in which these activities are going to take place.

Chapter Four

MAJOR COMMUNITY RESOURCES

Continuing in the spirit of "Where do we go from here," we can now begin to isolate the major resource groups that are common to most large cities. Here is where the information is; here are the resource personnel who can answer pointed questions authoritatively; and often, as current slang would have it, here is where the action is.

With so much community organization centering about these groups and their activities, the obviousness of establishing some type of relationship with them on the part of the school is clear.

The organizations which appear here were chosen because they are present in one form or another in most of the metropolitan areas in this country. In each instance, there is a section on information available. It is hoped that in highlighting such material, we have helped those who, for lack of experience, would not know exactly what resources these groups are likely to possess. Most organizations will be happy to furnish this type of information if it is requested.

CHAMBER OF COMMERCE

Although the Chamber is essentially dedicated to the economic development of a community, it usually takes an active interest in many phases of the city's life. It will work with other institutions in order to improve the image of the city or its services to people so that new businesses will want to move into the area.

The Chamber conducts special studies on many problems of urban community and provides commercial enterprises with materials for long-range planning. A Chamber is usually composed of several departments with subcommittees, usually oriented around certain projects in which the Chamber is engaged. Typical departments and committees are:

a) Aviation, Transportation and World Trade Departments

b) Industrial Development and Business Research Departments

c) Business and Industrial Relations and Civic Affairs Departments (departments such as these will deal especially with labor relations, national affairs, state legislation, civic and educational affairs)

d) Membership Department

e) Education Committee

f) Convention Department

g) Public Relations Department

h) Labor Relations Department

i) Safety Committee

In addition to much "city beautiful" material, some of which may be useful in determining part of the community's self-image, the Chamber will usually provide:

a) statistics (demographic, employment, lists of educational facilities and enrollments, tax rates)

b) a general history of the city
c) a list of city officials
d) a directory of manufacturers in the area
e) a directory of labor union officials in the area
f) lists of trade and other professional organizations
g) lists of advertising agencies, attorneys, real estate dealers, manufacturers' representatives, employment agencies, and accountants

The Chamber will regularly revise and publish its annual report, a program of work or resumé of activities, complete with future plans of each of the departments mentioned above and names of key men in each department, and some form of magazine. In some cases, the Chamber will make a film of its program of work and would be willing to show and explain it to the student body.

Each business and industry of the city typically sends one representative to participate in Chamber activities. Nonprofit organizations may also become members of the Chamber. The company pays dues according to the number of employees and a member, if elected by the majority of the members, might serve as an officer. Usually, dues and company donations provide the resources for Chamber activities.

Special Viewpoint

The Chamber's position on any question is determined by how the outcome will affect the business in the city and the image of the city. The Chamber may sponsor a cultural event so that the city may become a renowned cultural center, for example. Any program or project which will aid the economic development of a city will be sponsored, directed or at least influenced by the Chamber.

Contact

Usually, the Chamber will have full-time office personnel: executive director or secretary, public relations director, and secretaries. The public relations director is usually an excellent source for obtaining information.

COMMUNITY STUDIES ORGANIZATIONS

Organized for the purpose of performing research studies on local governmental problems in an urban community, a community research organization may appear as part of the Chamber activity or may be a distinct but allied organization.

Corporations of this type, once rare, are beginning to become standard fixtures of our great urban communities. Titles may differ, such as Metropolitan Community Studies or Community Research, but the basic structure of a private nonprofit organization will be found in many large cities. These offices are supported by private contributions, not connected with any political party or local government, and concern themselves with conducting research on metropolitan problems.

Under its regulations, the corporation is not permitted to engage in any promotional or political action programs. It does make its reports and studies available to the public, to local governmental officials, and to interested groups.

Most states have a governmental research bureau at

the main state university. The bureau traditionally makes studies of the urban communities within the state boundaries and often makes them available to the public. Consultants from such bureaus are available to private organizations on a contract basis. Similar research facilities exist in some states as part of a legislative reference and research office, and sometimes their studies and reports are made available to the public through members of the state legislature.

GOVERNMENT PLANNING BOARDS

Planning boards usually are of three types: city, county and regional. City and county planning boards are planning and advisory bodies composed of a small group of citizens appointed by the city or county commission or the mayor. Served by a full-time staff and a full-time planning director, the planning board deals with zoning, land use, subdivision regulations, capital improvement programming, urban redevelopment, housing, traffic and thoroughfare planning. Charged with guiding and controlling the public and private physical development of the city and its environs, the board usually works from a master plan which tries to anticipate area needs well in advance.

Regional planning boards, cutting across many government jurisdictions, are served with a full-time staff of professional planners and usually center their attention on metropolitan transportation problems and development.

Planning boards deal with community problems of a physical nature in their broadest contexts while other agencies are more specific and therefore much more likely to be the scene of coordination between the school and civic arena. Several kinds of information, however, are especially good in getting a concrete picture of the physical-spatial layout of the city. Such information as

a) regional transportation plans
b) employment trends and distribution surveys
c) inner city redevelopment programs
d) population and growth perspectives
e) urban development perspectives
f) housing studies

will do much in the early stages of learning about a community to concretize a picture of the layout of the civic arena in the minds of students and faculty. Many planning boards have excellent maps that are invaluable — base maps of the city and county, district and census tracts, industrial land use, zoning, and maps reflecting the economic and social conditions of the community.

Competent developers and trained staff make up the actual planning staff of most boards. The citizen group, usually concerned with policy, consists of businessmen and representatives of key industries. A call to the planning director or his administrative assistant will place you in touch with the planning office.

DEPARTMENT OF URBAN RENEWAL

Since 1948, when the need for some type of urban redevelopment was recognized by Congress, city after city has set up an urban renewal agency. This department is usually directly responsible to the city manager or mayor, and consists of a full-time staff which works jointly with the city planning board as part of the organization of the city government. The urban renewal department, where it exists, will conduct a program involving three different types of urban renewal projects, all of which may be involved in a single program: redevelopment, rehabilitation, and conservation.

Redevelopment consists in the acquisition of all or nearly all of a project area which is then cleared of housing and buildings. Street layouts are redesigned; public facilities are installed; and land is reserved for such construction as schools, recreational areas, parks, new housing, and new businesses. Land is then sold for these specific land uses based upon the predetermined plan.

Rehabilitation, involving as little land acquisition as possible, consists mainly in upgrading what structures are already in an area. A sound minimum housing ordinance and the constant and consistent cooperation of residents and absolute necessities for such a program. For students, such programs open up large areas of involvement in neighborhoods undergoing rehabilitation. Neighborhood "clean-up, fix-up" campaigns, helping residents to beautify their homes, are projects which can be developed.

Conservation areas are ones in which conditions, now rather decent, are deteriorating. Different kinds of people have moved into an area, usually from lower income brackets. Unless conditions are to become disastrous, neighborhood involvement and action aimed at stabilizing the area are necessary. Hence, the name conservation.

The major problem with urban renewal seems to be people! Families in a redevelopment area are dispossessed of housing and aid is given to them to help them find new housing. Often, the neighborhoods into which these families are relocated begin to deteriorate themselves and the process is repeated. Part of the relocation program of the urban renewal department should be a social service and counseling program to deal with family problems uncovered by urban renewal.

Any urban renewal department will have such materials as:

a) complete listings and profiles of urban renewal projects and surrounding community conditions;

b) pamphlets on various urban renewal services, especially relocation booklets and social service guides;

c) fact sheets on housing put out by the Federal Department of Housing and Urban Development;

d) complete sets of community development plans, similar to those available from the planning boards; and

e) article reprints concerning various aspects of urban renewal.

A professionally trained staff of planners, case workers and public and private personnel are engaged in various aspects of the urban renewal program. Case workers and public and private welfare workers may be involved in the social service aspects of the department's activities.

In many cities urban renewal has stimulated the development of neighborhood agencies and centers as residents sought to cooperate with the urban renewal program. In these centers many projects are organized which are in need of volunteers of high school age.

Teachers should be well aware that neighborhood centers are prime contacts for the development of action programs.

COMMUNITY WELFARE ORGANIZATIONS

In most of our larger cities, some type of federated organization exists which provides its member organizations with funds, research and planning in the operation of community welfare. Its membership consists of both tax-supported and voluntary organizations, as well as the major professional associations in the social service field, usually with a considerable number of civic institutions. This type of organization serves as a coordinating body for the innumerable agencies dealing with health, welfare and recreation. Most of the time it is privately financed and the bulk of its money comes from the Red Feather fund-raising program.

Similar to the Chamber of Commerce, control of a community welfare council is vested in a body of delegates from the member organizations, from which a board of directors is chosen. In turn, this board sets policy for the entire welfare program of the area. The binding power of this policy-making group on the private institutions within the organizations varies from city to city. It is significant to know that board members are men and women prominent in business and civic organizations, clergymen, and educators, as well as professional social workers. The staff will include an executive director, a director of research, several social workers, program planners, fund-raising personnel, secretaries and clerks.

Usually, a community organization of this type serves a variety of functions. At the request of member agencies or other responsible organizations, the organization will review existing community service programs and assist agencies in reshaping programs to meet new needs. Also, the council will plan and promote new programs for the community. For example, in the face of the rapidly increasing number of older people, community welfare councils have assisted in the organization of senior citizen centers in many cities. The community welfare council serves continuously as a major channel for voluntary coordination of private and public agencies concerned with social welfare and problems of the community. Such a group as this usually does not seek to control member agencies' programs.

Another function is the processing of material which is of value in the planning and development of community service and the arrangement of special studies related to health, welfare and recreation. The council may sponsor neighborhood and local community organizations, sometimes helping in the actual organization of such groups by providing staff assistance.

When such a council or federation exists in the city, it can provide a wealth of information valuable for a clear picture of the urban community. Such material is available as:

a) booklets describing the council and the local Red Feather agency; their functions, resources, programs, member agencies, structure of the organization;

b) lists of the members of the board of directors and

agency representatives;

c) annual report to the members, listing various services, plans and future projects as well as reports of past activities;

d) summary lists of local governmental structures and personnel;

e) booklets on such subjects as family and children's services, services for the blind, services for youth, etc.;

f) comprehensive surveys on social service programs in the city;

g) studies done in conjunction with colleges and universities;

h) outlines of federal programs such as the War on Poverty which are operating in the area.

Occasionally, an attempt is made to inventory systematically the social characteristics (the socio-economic indices) of each census tract in the area. Such social profiles are not commonly comprehensive, but most councils will at least have census material organized into profiles for small areas, usually slums or other areas slated for redevelopment.

The executive director of the community coordinating council is perhaps the best man to see in this case. He will be well aware of all the studies and reports made, and of planned and ongoing programs, and conscious of internal problems among various agencies making up the coordinating body. He also can be quite helpful in singling out member agencies needing volunteer services and could show where a school program could fit into the complete program of the council. Contacts can also be made with the heads of any one of the affiliated agencies and neighborhood organizations. If the school comes with specific requests for cooperation, it is often possible to get some advice and planning help from the council staff. In several instances, community welfare councils have provided personnel to Catholic high schools for conducting orientation programs for students who were going to be placed in volunteer work. In one city, the local council's volunteer placement bureau arranged for a member agency (the local chapter of the social work professional association) to conduct orientation programs for students, help prepare faculty moderators, and help place students with agencies with programs that would make the best use of them.

COMMUNITY CHEST — RED FEATHER

The Community Chest, serving the community principally as a fund raiser and disburser, unites the appeals and campaigns of its Red Feather agencies, although usually the Chest does not attempt to set policy for the agencies for which it raises funds. Of necessity, the board of the Community Chest is made up of the leading bankers, industrialists, and merchants in the community.

THE PUBLIC LIBRARY

It should be noted that many times the reference sections of public libraries, Chambers of Commerce, and planning commissions have many publications dealing with the census. Public libraries in large cities often are centers for storing federal documents and thus have much material of this kind. Census material for each

Standard Metropolitan Area is available separately. If all else fails, sets of tables and charts can be obtained from the government by writing the Superintendent of Documents, Government Printing Office, Washington, D. C. 20025. Area offices of the Department of Commerce usually have much of the same information.

Population charts and graphs for Standard Metropolitan Areas, age group listings, social characteristics of an area such as racial distribution, marital status, employment indices and opportunities, household relationships, education, mobility of families, family income, labor force potentialities, census tract information, are all available from the Census Bureau.

The public library of any good-sized city will be a valuable asset in studying the community. Most public libraries will place local materials in a special department. If it does not, the reference room of the library will double as the city room.

The materials available will differ to quite a large extent, depending upon such factors as the policy of the library and the interest and involvement of the library in local affairs. Much of the available material will duplicate what local agencies have, of course, but older and out-of-print reports can often be found only in the public library. It goes without saying that students should be familiar with their local library facilities.

THE NEWSPAPER MORGUE

Each newspaper keeps records of its back issues. Sometimes this amounts to a simple chronological collection, but more often it involves the filing of individual articles according to subjects and names of people and organizations. Along with this is usually a complete index to the clipping file. This is the newspaper morgue. It should be noted that very few local papers are indexed.

Usually the morgue is semiprivate, but in general, admission can be gained by a telephone call to the newspaper librarian explaining the reasons for the use of the morgue — study projects, research on city government, etc. A second alternative is to contact a reporter or editor, explain the project, and ask admittance into the morgue. After a few visits, it might be possible to drop in any time. Students use is usually restricted.

One of the most important benefits of the morgue is that it allows one to trace the activities of individual persons or organizations over a period of years. This type of information is helpful in gaining an indication of the activities, experiences, and programs of a group, perhaps in preparing an approach to the organization or an idea of which organizations in the city are active, which the influential in certain arenas of community decisions, and which might wish to work with teenage youngsters.

LEAGUE OF WOMEN VOTERS

The League of Women Voters is a nonpartisan organization working to inform citizens about government and community issues related in some way to legislation. Its main function is to conduct intensive studies and to publish reports. The League holds general membership meetings (often non-members are welcome to sit in on these sessions) and neighborhood discussion meetings. Usually, the League maintains a Speakers' Bureau and issues a candidates' bulletin for the public before the general elections. Fact sheets on issues and amendments on the ballot are also published. It is important to note that the League will never support candidates for office and does not endorse any side of an issue.

The National League of Women Voters conducts and publishes studies on federal legislation. In order to receive its charter, each local branch is required to complete and keep updated a local government, town and township, and local county study. Also, the organization in each area is likely to have:

a) programs on its annual activities;

b) school survey guides (questions on school organization and activities) ;

c) fact books about the League of Women Voters;

d) an analysis of the community, including a history of the town; geographical analysis; population analysis; political, economic, social, civic, educational and welfare characteristics and resources;

e) reports on blighted areas within the city and county;

f) local school and government studies;

g) information on education beyond the high school, needs of the community in this respect, and potential resources for post-high school educational facilities.

A few local leagues also have information on the local advertising and communication media.

It is useful to keep in mind that the League — and

many others of the organizations discussed here — will be reluctant to send much more than brochures and other printed information if they receive a request for it through the mails. Yet, these agencies will be most cooperative if they are contacted personally and asked first hand for specific information. This is the best way to find out about any aspect of the city: personal contact.

CHURCH ORGANIZATIONS
Protestant Church Groups

In our larger urban areas, a new type of service organization has come into exisence representing most of the Protestant denominations in the area, coordinating the work of ministerial associations, lay organizations, Christian education, publicity, weekday church schools, overseas relief work, institutional ministries, leadership training and social and welfare programs. It offers such services as collecting and publicizing information about Protestant churches, church leaders and program activities. These church federations conduct research and surveys for the member churches and coordinate planning for member churches.

Protestant church federations are policy-making groups but their decisions are not binding on member churches. Individual churches may (and often do) take different positions with regard to social questions than the church federation itself, for example. This is why many civil rights groups often treat federation statements as mere words.

A federation is usually headed by an executive body which is made up of elected officials, past presidents, department chairmen, denominational representatives, community organization representatives, and members-at-large.

The organization is usually made up of departments such as the following:

a) administration (business and finance; personnel; goals and evaluation committee, nominating committee)

b) Christian education (youth work committee, family life and life and leadership training committees)

c) Christian life and work (intercultural affairs, social welfare, church and public affairs, church and economic life committees)

d) church extension and special ministries (chaplaincy and pastoral services committee, ministerial associations committee, cooperative church planning committee)

e) public relations (public information committee, press, radio and television committee)

Depending on local diocesan policies, Catholic representatives may or may not be found on various committees. It is not unusual to find Catholic observers attending meetings, however, and when local policy permits this, the Catholic high school can profit tremendously from having a representative in a position to know what areas of cooperation can be explored. Various youth projects sponsored by the church federations are very suitable for Catholic student participation.

While church federations are not found in every community, even very small cities will have a Protestant ministerial association. There will be either denominational association (Baptist, Lutheran, Methodist) or interdenominational. While the church federation essentially is oriented to the socio-civic order, the ministerial association coordinates pastoral functions and church activities, and helps to alleviate pastoral problems common to member denominations. Of course, where church federations are not present, the ministerial association will often take up the work the federation might otherwise do. In many areas, the Catholic clergy are members of the ministerial groups.

Information is available on the work of the church federation and/or ministerial association and any research which is conducted by or for these groups. Newsletters, bibliographies, and project reports are often valuable.

A very good policy is for teachers to visit the pastors of various Protestant churches. Often, too much of a wall exists between Catholic educators and the leaders of the Protestant community. Common programs can often be worked out and appearances both in the Catholic school by the Protestant clergy and visitations of Catholic educators to Protestant Sunday-School sessions can be arranged.

The American Friends' Service Committee, a Quaker social-welfare group, is prominent in social and civic activities. Familiarity with its work will help to round out one's view of the Protestant community.

Along this line, although not traditionally identified as Protestant, the Unitarian church generally is the most socially conscious of the religious groups in the community. Quite liberal in their orientation, the Unitarians have special programs for young people.

Catholic Charities

Usually the dominant social welfare agency in the Catholic community, Catholic Charities provides family and children services for Catholic individuals and families. Casework and consultation service in marital and family difficulties, in budgeting and homemaking, and for problems arising from mental and physical illness, forms the bulk of the organization's activities. Services are also given in parent-child relationships, to unmarried parents in need of assistance for themselves or placement for their children, and to individuals having personality difficulties. Catholic Charities acts as an agent for state welfare departments in the recommendation for foster-care homes, and usually handles adoptions for Catholic families. Sometimes, the agency participates in federal programs.

Case workers usually are college graduates, working mothers, and volunteers having limited preparation for their employment as case workers. Usually a priest is director of the agency and although funds are usually diocesan and Red Feather, they seldom meet all the pressing needs. In organization, staff, and types of activities, Catholic Charities offices differ little from public agencies. An easy liaison between them and the Catholic school system makes them an obvious contact for student volunteer work, however.

Jewish Community Council

Often unknown to Catholic teachers raised in a conservative family and religious background, the Jewish Community Council provides casework and group work service for the Jewish community, including family, counseling and financial assistance, foster care and adoption services, care to the aged, leisure time and recreational programs, and community and human relations programs. Such councils, allied with Jewish community centers and local synagogues, often participate in legislative and educational programs in the fields of civil liberties, housing, fair employment, censorship and freedom of speech, and public education. Jewish Community Council public relations programs aim at a development of better religious and cultural relations among community citizens. The council is supported in most cases by the Community Chest and the United Jewish Appeal.

Information on the Jewish community comes primarily from newsletters relating to the work of the council and affairs within the Jewish community, Jewish community newspapers, publications from national organizations such as the National Jewish Congress, National Jewish Committee, and the Anti-Defamation League of B'nai B'rith.

Contacts can be made with the executive director, who usually is an experienced professional, and with the head of the community relations committee or the head of the Jewish family service.

American Judaism contains three religious groupings: Orthodox, Conservative, and Reformed (sometimes called Liberal).

The Orthodox Jew regards his faith as part of an unalterable tradition stretching back thousands of years and made rich by the heritage of many men. To alter the form of faith is unheard of among the strictly Orthodox. On social questions, the Orthodox Jew is usually more conservative than either his Conservative or Reformed brethren. For example, Orthodox Jews seek to train their children in their own private religious schools rather than allow the children to go to public school.

The Conservative Jew regards Judaism as an ever-changing, evolving religion. Many of the religious patterns held sacred by the Orthodox, such as strict observance of the Sabbath, are considered outmoded by the Conservative, who also does not follow the traditional dietary rules strictly.

Reform Judaism differs sharply from the other branches — the worship service of a Reform Jew departs quite radically from traditional forms, and customs that he believes not adapted to modern times are regarded as useless by the Reform Jew.

It is impossible, as it was with Protestants, and increasingly so with Catholics, to determine one point of view within the Jewish community. Usually the Jewish community will be politically liberal, although it is true that the Conservative, Orthodox, and Reform disagree on social questions quite sharply. A clue (and that is all it is) of the view of the Jewish community can be garnered from determining which is the dominant group in the Jewish community.

THE SCHOOL BOARD

The general public elects a school board which then

appoints a superintendent of schools and a number of assistants who aid him in his work. The Board of Education supervises and administers all the public schools in the district in all phases of school activity. Through the principal which it appoints, the Board controls the policy of each public school.

Every education office is composed of various departments which offer services to public schools in the district. In many cases, audio-visual supplies, visiting nurses and other services are available to private schools. Such departments include a school and community relations committee which maintains contacts with local communication media for disseminating information about schools and for evaluating community reactions to programs, and an instruction committee which conducts a continuous program of curriculum revision. This last group often conducts seminars for teachers, principals, and supervisors. A research staff will do basic studies to provide statistics on population, census material, information on the latest laws touching schools, and trends in salaries and benefits. City school systems maintain audio-visual offices which offer films, tapes, and records for each school. In addition, two other committees are usually found as extensions of the school board: an athletic committee to establish policy concerning interscholastic sports, and a pupil personnel department to provide counselors, school psychologists, and special diagnostic services for each school. It works with city health officials regarding health of school children. A special function of this committee is the investigation of cases requiring home or hospital tutoring and the secur-

ing of teachers for this purpose. Many of the auxiliary
services of public schools systems are available to
Catholic schools.

Too often, Catholic schools neglect contact with public
schools, perhaps through a sense of rivalry, perhaps
through distrust and fear. Yet, there is a multitude of
opportunities for concrete, meaningful programs which
can be worked out in conjunction with the public
schools. The school system usually is an excellent resource; for one thing, it is usually a major local agent
for federal and state programs for youth. Perhaps some
of the tensions would ease if both realized that essentially
they are in the same business — educating the community's youth and bettering the community's education. Catholics have rarely thought in this dimension,
and both faculty and parents may have to be re-educated
in this direction.

Most public school systems offer a general teacher's
guide from which much basic information can be
obtained. Materials are available on adult educational
programs, vocational education, summer school and
tutoring programs, participation in antipoverty projects,
copies of curriculum revisions, and policies of the use
of school grounds and facilities.

Due to the poverty program, the school board and the
individual district schools are relating to the community
on more and more projects by such means as human
relations institutes and forums for teachers and administrators. In this respect, the Detroit Public School System
has recently published an impressive guide for the formation of human relations clubs, including a description

of resources in Detroit for such clubs and lists of contacts for teachers interested in forming such clubs.

It is important to understand that the school board does in large measure control policy for district schools and teachers. Sometimes, Catholic schools may find individual schools and teachers reluctant to cooperate in projects and programs. Often, this is not due to the policy of the individual school or teacher, but the general policy of the board of education. Various influences, especially political ones, often hinder public schools from free participation in community programs that are in any way controversial.

THE URBAN LEAGUE

The Urban League has been described as an interracial agency that gathers and interprets economic and sociological facts on conditions among racial minorities. Its main focus is on job opportunities for the Negro. It provides placement, job counseling, occupational information services to minority group youth and vocational guidance to all young people. Maintaining a Speakers' Bureau, the Urban League distributes literature and conducts annual human relations institutes as a means of improving intergroup relations. This agency will cooperate with other agencies in the city on common problems. One of the League's greatest accomplishments in many cities is the opening of employment opportunities for Negroes by negotiating with local businesses.

Annual reports, pamphlets on all phases of interracial and intergroup relationships, publications resulting from various special nationally sponsored assemblies, and complete lists of bibliographical material relating to youth incentives and education are all available from local League offices.

The Urban League does not regard itself as a civil-rights action group, but as an agency devoted to supplying the basic research, talent and methods necessary for the improvement of race relations within the existing structure of society. It deals with management, labor, and public officials to achieve the gradual alleviation of some of the worst aspects of minority status. For this reason, many militant Negroes regard the League with distrust.

HUMAN RELATIONS COMMISSION

In certain large cities, a human relations commission or a council on human affairs exists to promote better relations among various cultural, racial, ethnic, social and religious groups in the community. It is usually part of the local governmental structure, but sometimes appears as a privately organized and financed group, similar to many other community social agencies. It is not a civil rights group (although many people may think of it as such) but serves as an advisory body to governmental, civic, and business groups on matters having to do with intergroup relations. Assistance is given in the form of legislative drafting, educational programs to promote better racial and cultural relations among groups, and to ministers, teachers, and social workers in dealing with the problems in intergroup relations. A special function of a governmental commission is to receive and investigate complaints of violations of laws dealing with human relations. Cooperation is given to federal, state and local agencies in the enforcement of such laws. A major function of the groups, whether public or private, is to help conflicting groups.

A board of directors ordinarily serves as the policy-making body of the commission. The chairman and board members may serve without pay and the composition of the board significantly represents the Protestant, Catholic, Jewish, Negro, management, labor, and other groups in the city.

Committees might include executive, program, education, public relations, community relations and service committees. Structure varies widely, depending on whether the group is a public agency or privately directed.

FURTHER NOTES ON SOME RESOURCES
Civil Rights Groups

Although they are not strictly resource organizations, it is advisable to check into the spectrum of civil rights groups in the local community. This can be done by checking the local newspaper for names of active groups, or by asking the executive director of a human relations or community welfare agency for a list of such organizations. Contacting these groups is valuable to understanding, for each takes a different perspective on the question of interracial justice, a perspective it would be important to know about if any activity is contemplated in this field.

Groups of this nature that are usually found in most cities include:

a) National Association for Advancement of Colored People — the oldest and best established group, approaching civil rights from a broad, legal perspective with some orientation to direct action.

b) Congress of Racial Equality — a more militant group, pledged to the concept of direct action against the community power structure, using direct action if necessary.

c) Southern Christian Leadership Conference — traditionally oriented to voter registration drives and peaceful marches, the Conference has moved north to begin massive improvement programs for the northern city slums.

d) Catholic Interracial Council — more active in the East than elsewhere, the C.I.C. centers its activity in providing education programs, tutoring and group discussion programs. It often cooperates with other civil rights groups on specific projects rather than initiating its own. It sponsors Junior C.I.C. groups for teenagers, and helps establish them in Catholic high schools.

e) Student Nonviolent Coordinating Committee — a predominantly Southern, student volunteer agency, S.N.C.C.'s major activity centers in the "Black Belts" of the South. Student groups called Friends of S.N.C.C. appear on northern campuses. It engages in direct action programs such as voter registration, political party organization, and it is often antagonistic toward moderate solutions to civil rights problems.

Political Parties

The purpose of political parties is to run men for office and to enable them to win. The local branches of the Republican and Democratic parties are important organizations to come into contact with, but it is important to understand the relative amount of influence the parties have in the community. In many cases, especially in the East, domination of a city by a political party is the common pattern. In cities having a council-manager form of government, however, the parties often are not so dominant, since candidates often must be nonpartisan to run for council positions. Political parties are not a major resource organization for the school in the usual sense. If they are willing to part with them, parties usually have study profiles of various neighborhoods on hand.

The Local University

The local university or college is an excellent resource center. University departments such as sociology, political science, or public administration are called upon by cities to do basic research for government and industry, and in many cases, the community research organization will be located at one of the area universities.

Human relations centers, community-wide forums on community issues, and educational television programs are among the breakthroughs by which the university is serving the local community.

In any urban community of some size, there are literally hundreds of resource groups to help the teacher become familiar with his community. In one moderate-sized midwestern city, one school found over two hundred distinct organizations in the field of welfare alone! An almost endless list could be made — the organizations chosen for spotlighting here are those which are consistently found in most urban areas. City-wide youth councils, police athletic leagues, Catholic youth organizations, and boys' clubs, are other groups with which profitable relationships can and should be established by the Catholic high school.

The local branch of the Y.M.C.A. or Y.W.C.A. is usually a very fine resource organization. In some areas of the country, a certain narrow-mindedness (on both sides) must be shaken off before meaningful cooperation can take place between a local Catholic high school and the "Y." In the area of leadership training especially, the "Y" is a great help to a faculty member.

Two other groups should be mentioned: neighborhood centers and volunteer service bureaus. The former provide a tremendous amount of information on a given neighborhood and are traditionally organized to use volunteers of high school age. In many cities, a volunteer service center acts as a clearing house for volunteer organizations in the city. Such a center will alert agencies in need of volunteers and will place volunteers in programs. In many cases they offer an orientation program to volunteers who are giving of their time and service. For a high school teacher needing to place students in a volunteer project, contact with a volunteer service organization is tremendously valuable for studying the range of opportunities available and suitable for student activity.

PART II
ACTION PROGRAMS

ACTION PROGRAMS

On the pages that follow are listed examples of different programs which are underway in various high schools throughout the country. They are designed to demonstrate different programs in different types of situations and to illustrate the various possibilities that exist for developing the relationship between existing school programs and the civic community.

It is important to understand at the outset that involving students in activities does not insure formation in social responsibility or even growth in appreciation of the Christian's apostolic commitment to Christianize society. Even granting that the teenager cannot formulate a complete Christian orientation towards life until he or she is more mature, still the teachers and moderators of projects must attempt to form the student in distinctly Christian attitudes through individual guidance and counseling. Involvement in activity is important and necessary as a supplement to the classroom, but involvement alone does not insure continued growth in developing a Christian personality. This point, seemingly so obvious, is often overlooked by moderators overly involved in the details of setting up and organizing projects.

These action programs are in many instances undergoing evolution and development. They are all in existence, however, and have had varying amounts of success. Similar, though not identical, programs can be set up in almost any school with a competent faculty willing to sacrifice the extra time and effort which such projects demand.

Program One
DEVELOPING A PROGRAM
FROM A PROBLEM STUDY

In many instances one is aware of a specific problem without a clear notion of how it can or should be approached. Perhaps some tentative solutions have been reached theoretically, and it seems that the problem, or some aspects of it, can be effectively approached by students. The specific task, therefore, becomes one of finding ways for students to become actively involved in confronting the problem.

If the problem has been identified through a problem census or some other class procedure, the first steps will be undertaken within the classroom. Presuming that the problem fits into the syllabus of the course and has some relevance, it may be discussed, the background explored, and some reading done on the subject. The teacher should be aware of the fact, however, that if and when the students begin working actively on some aspect of a problem outside of class time, their interest will deepen considerably, and they will keep bringing the problem back to the classroom for further discussion and study. Without discouraging this result of heightened motivation, the teacher must gently avoid allowing a single issue to dominate the class for a long period. Each teacher will have to make the judgment about class balance for himself.

There are essentially two types of programs that can ordinarily be approached. One would involve an in-school operation exclusively, in which the social problem (presumably directly involving the school) will be attacked through some part of the school structure. This type of thing is done every time a guidance program for special students is set up, or some traditional part of the institution is mobilized to meet a need that arises. The interest of these Action Programs lies in those aspects that are amenable to student participation. If the ordinary operations of the school are functioning well, it will be unusual that student participation will prove very valuable, but only a study of the nature of the problem will indicate the approach that is proper in every instance.

With an in-school program, the first step is to determine whether or not an existing school agency (perhaps a club) is capable of dealing with the problem. If so, perhaps the solution lies simply in motivating the interested students to become active in the group and help it discover a solution. In this way, for example, a C.Y.O. might be brought to provide greater recreational opportunities for the teenagers of an area. In another situation, a Junior Interracial Council which has been largely a study group might be brought to deal with the problem of rejection of Negro students in the school.

If an existing group is not available, either a club or some type of student committee can be set up, perhaps under the aegis of the Student Council. Whenever possible, not only faculty, but also parents should be involved.

The second type of program directly involves agencies in the community. If the problem is a significant one, there will probably be some public or voluntary group that deals with the question. The initial step would then be to establish a contact with the proper group, and this contact should be made by the teacher and not by a student. It goes without saying that the school administration has been consulted and kept informed of all developments. After all, the school name and public image are connected to any program involving its students.

Since many agencies have had little or no experience in dealing with youngsters, the teacher should try to find a person who is in charge of youth work, if the particular agency has any such staff member. The purpose of the initial contact is to make an offer of cooperation, and to try to explore areas in which high-school students might be of value. Someone within the organization should be chosen by the agency as being responsible from the agency's side for the student participation program. This gives the teacher an immediate contact who will always know what is going on. This person may also be useful in recruiting participants by giving talks in classes, meeting with clubs or other groups, etc. A former teacher will often be most cooperative.

The placement of students is a crucial point. The moderator needs to know them well enough to place them where they will do the best job, and learn the most. A student should never be given an assignment, no matter how enthusiastic he is, that he is incompetent to under-

take. This raises a controversial issue: what type of stu
dent should be allowed into any program of participation.
Recruitment cannot be so general that anyone can take
part indiscriminately. If there is a large and well-
developed program, places can be found for the likely
lad who is willing but needs constant supervision and
cannot contribute much. Ordinarily, however, and especially when programs are getting started, the students
must be chosen carefully and placed carefully. A student
should be willing to prove himself; the youngster who
turns up for a day or so and then drops out, is too un-
reliable. As a program expands, place may be found for
this type in recreational activities with small children,
working with retarded children, and other activities
where there is ready supervision, and continuity is not
at a premium.

Even when supervision is provided regularly, the
school moderator should "drop by" occasionally to check
students in the program. Beyond this, his main task is to
maintain an evaluation program on a regular basis.
Personal contacts and interviews enable the teacher to
judge the student's experience, and allow the student
himself to articulate his experience. By doing this, he
can strengthen his motivation and thrash out any difficulties that seem to be developing. This evaluation will
happen much more naturally if the teacher himself is
taking part in the program with the students. The
teacher's attitudes will be colored by his own experiences,
but this need not be a hindering factor, unless a discipline problem with the students arises. Regular contact
with the agency representative must be kept up through-

out the process, of course.

Adolescents, especially boys, seem to have the attitude that their parents are not too interested in their activities. The parents should be completely informed of any program in which their sons and daughters are taking part, and preferably should be asked to sign a statement that they are aware of what is involved. An orientation meeting for parents is a good idea, and it is an effective means of recruiting help from them as well. Often, school systems require some type of release form as a condition of participation in any school activity, so many schools will already have a standard procedure for obtaining parental approval.

A clear understanding should be reached between school and agency about what will happen when school closes for the summer. If the program is a year-round one, there is the obvious question of how students will be able to continue to offer their services. This type of thing should be foreseen.

Many of the Action Programs outlined here illustrate various approaches to particular problems that have been undertaken.

Program Two

PUBLIC RELATIONS

Few people in America are ignorant of the fact that the Catholic Church maintains a school system separate from the one attended by the majority of American school children. Over the past few years, non-Catholics and Catholics who do not send their children to parochial schools have learned a good deal more about the Catholic school system. Yet, in many minds, the description of a Catholic school as a divisive educational system serving the Catholic community still is the image. Exceptions exist, of course, but even many Catholic school administrators themselves conceive of the Catholic school as separate from the rest of the community. This tendency, naturally enough, seems in inverse proportion to the level of Catholic education: Catholic colleges are, and must be, involved with the local community much more than the grade or high schools.

Many high schools have begun to arrest the tendency to remain outside the pale of community activities in at least one significant area: cooperation with local public school systems to improve the educational facilities of the Catholic schools. This is an important first step and should be pursued, but even here the emphasis is on what a community agency can do for the school and not vice versa. Such considerations are necessary and cannot be forgotten (especially when finances tend to be limited) , but they project a negative image of the school to the community. In short, the service aspect of the Catholic school has not been emphasized. Our parochial schools have failed to build a reputation as excellent schools with a competent faculty which is serving the community through education, religion, and civic concern.

We have stressed here the conception of a Catholic high school conscious of its obligation to provide a service to the local community — that of preparing its students with an education which includes moral and social formation of a high calibre. A high school which graduates students who have been well-educated and who are keenly socially conscious, and which has cooperated with community agencies to form these students, has done a great service for any community. At the same time, a high school which has faculty members on its staff who are willing to be actively and competently involved in civic affairs again is doing a great deal for a city. Perhaps this is the emphasis which administrators of Catholic schools should focus upon. Perhaps, then, public relations for any Catholic high school consists in forming in the community at large — and among certain subgroups in that community — the image of a school fully devoted to the improvement of education for all the students in an urban community with an emphasis upon the moral and social aspects of education.

Such image building is a delicate task, and many times is accompanied by the strange and uncomfortable sensation that no one really knows what the image of the school is, even after a lot of work has been done.

Often, public relations must begin among faculty members, some of whom may conceive of publicity as something faintly disreputable and smacking of a huckster approach to education. Through a faculty orientation program early in the year and through continuing faculty meetings teachers can be exposed to the reasons behind various public relations programs. All members should be kept informed of the publicity which the school receives. Students should be kept abreast of this publicity as well, possibly through the use of a centrally-located bulletin board.

Special care should be taken to report only programs and events which are actually happening and to represent these accurately. Realism and sincerity are guide words to intelligent public relations. At the same time, all programs, activities, special courses in all fields of endeavor — educational, apostolic, social, cultural and athletic — should be given as much coverage as is reasonable and possible.

Depending upon local conditions and special considerations, certain aspects of the school and its program will need emphasis. In most high schools, athletic events are well publicized; in many schools, the educational curriculum is highly regarded and some schools are noted for the excellent cultural programs they sponsor. In many cities, Catholic high schools are well known and widely supported by the Catholic community. This is not always the case, however. The educational community is well aware of the school's existence in many cities; in other areas it is not. Few are the cities in which the civic community as a whole is aware of, or interested in the local Catholic high schools, except possibly in the sense that the community feels that a massive closing of Catholic schools would be a financial disaster.

Whatever the case, a reputation either must be built or rebuilt in the Catholic community, the educational community, and the rest of the civic community. The school must be known as one serving the total community by giving a solid education to its students, one which emphasizes moral and social formation, a school which contributes to the community on both faculty and student levels through involvement in the community.

A coordinator of public relations should be appointed by the principal of the school. If possible, his load of courses and extracurriculars should be lightened to some degree. He should represent the school and its objectives to the wider community through attendance at various educational meetings. He should keep informed of every activity in the school, should plan ahead for coverage of upcoming events, prepare copy for the press (both Catholic and secular) about all school activities, coordinate the development of official school publications, and at least assist in the nomination of faculty members to civic groups. An attempt should be made to form a student public relations committee and the public relations coordinator should be its moderator.

A Catholic high school's good relations with the Catholic community are often taken for granted. If the local pastors do not register any complaints, the school presumes that all is well. In this age of diocesan senates, lay school boards, and other newer forms of participation by the Catholic public, communication with the various segments of the Catholic community is easier than ever.

Successful programs have been set up in a number of cities for periodic "articulation conferences" in which Catholic elementary school faculties meet with the high school faculty to discuss curricula and other common problems and interests. By including parish clergy in these meetings, a further dimension for cooperation is added.

Cooperation with pastors might be intensified if, aside from invitations to dinners and to school functions cooperation could be begun on common difficulties. A very good example of this is the program which has been set up by the principal of one small high school in which the principals of the Catholic schools in the city and a lay faculty member from each, along with the local pastors and a lay assistant for each, make up a board which meets monthly to work out common problems, such as school enrollment and finances, apostolic activities, public relations, etc. If the principal meets with and works with the local grade school principals, possibilities for a more organized approach to education from grade school through high school exist. The techniques are as varied as the local situation. Variations on them and new techniques should always be developed.

Even where articulation between the high school and the Catholic elementary schools exists, real contact between parents and faculty is not strong. In many Catholic high schools, in fact, the Parent-Teachers Association is little more than an administration front for fund raising. Few Catholic high schools are active in seeking parent participation in policy making. Highly important changes regarding admissions policy, tuition increases, and building programs are commonly announced to parents as accomplished facts. Every Catholic high school, and every Catholic school system, is going to have to develop realistic means of contact with its most immediate public: the families whose children attend the schools.

The Catholic high school distinctly is an educational institution and as such should relate professionally to the educational institutions around it, especially the public school system but also local universities and colleges. The federal poverty program has accelerated movements in this direction. Shared facilities have also helped to tie the systems closer to each other, and shared time programs in some communities have developed the process even further. In terms of public relations, however, such simple things as placing public schools on mailing lists for school publications, and inviting members of the board of education or the superintendent of schools to speak to the student body, attendance at meetings of the board of education, attendance at local programs of the university, issuing invitations to school functions, and cooperation on teachers' institutes all can improve relationships with public school officials. Out of such beginnings, concrete cooperation can evolve which will try to solve problems facing both school systems. Involvement in activities such as membership in educational groups like the local chapter of the National

Educational Association, can develop a more meaningful relationship between the two school systems. Many other similar techniques can be used. Simple courtesy demands, in addition, that all policy decisions affecting public schools be discussed with them in advance of public announcements.

It should be obvious that many of the same public relations activities can take place in terms of the school's relationship to the rest of the civic community. Inviting civic leaders to speak to the students should become a regular feature of the school assembly program; the mailing of brochures and newsletters to groups and individuals should be done as a matter of course, especially if a faculty member or a group of students is involved in one of their programs. Attendance at functions of many civic groups by the principal or his representative should also be encouraged. An extremely worthwhile custom is to invite community groups to make use of school facilities. The principal of one high school, for example, has invited the Chamber of Commerce to make use of the school facilities for a program in practical politics sponsored by the Chamber. Many persons previously unaware of the school became familiar with Catholic schools for the first time, and the Chamber is planning to move the entire program to the school, renting its facilities. Immense good will has come from this simple venture.

Many groups have education committees attempting to relate realistically the educational aspect of a city's growth to other aspects of its growth. Having a membership on such boards is a distinct advantage to the parochial high school and also solidifies the image of the high school faculty as one interested in the welfare of the entire community.

News of school activities, the achievements of individuals, feature articles on the school's athletic, cultural, and social action programs should be given to the secular press. Most newspapers have local community sections and coverage of the school's activities will only be given if information is passed on to the press. Except in unusual circumstances, they cannot cover many school activities on their own. A certain persistence is necessary. Perhaps four or five news items will be sent to the editors before one is printed, and the editor is the final judge of newsworthiness.

Although some techniques have been given here, perhaps what is more necessary than the use of particular devices is the development of an attitude on the part of school administrators and faculty members by which they view public relations as an important aspect of the school program. If this mentality is developed, imagination and knowledge of the school will be used effectively enough.

Program Three
A SPEAKERS' SERIES

One of the easiest ways of introducing the student body, faculty, and parents to an awareness of the social dimension of Catholic education is to invite representatives of various agencies and organizations in the community to speak to these groups, to lead discussions, and to give a general orientation to the community. Programs such as these can serve as a general introduction to the urban community and its problems, and although much more involvement and work is necessary if a real social keenness is to develop, a lecture-discussion program is a good first step in the process.

Essential to the organization and development of an assembly program for students is a careful consideration of its purposes. In most cases, such programs are designed to introduce the civic community to the student, and to make him generally aware of the city in which he is living. Consequently, speakers should not dwell at length on particulars or unrelated detailed analyses and lengthy sidelights, but merely explain clearly an agency's function in the community, its relationship to other civic institutions, and one or two of its major problems. An attempt should always be made to relate the agency in some way to the student. Often, a valuable point for a speaker to bring out is his own personal reasons for being a member of this group and for serving the civic community. The ideal speaker is one who can communicate to the students his own feelings of urgency and his own personal commitment.

The head of the agency, its public relations officer, or a top assistant should be the type of person chosen. The moderator of the assembly program should meet personally with the representative of the agency to iron out difficulties and certain necessary details. A speaker should not be engaged only on a third person's recommendation. The speaker must be interesting and able to project his personality well. Boredom can set in rapidly if he is not.

Contacts with major resource organizations, attendance at various civic meetings, the reading of newspapers will provide a list of names from which to choose speakers. Prominent parents of students often can be the first to be sought out to speak and some of them, if told that the scope of the series of assembly programs is to inspire community awareness, will be able and willing to suggest potential speakers who are competent and interesting.

If well coordinated and worked out in advance, panel discussions are excellent, especially if they can be arranged on controversial issues such as federal aid to private schools, use of poverty funds, racial justice. Often, a valuable feature of panels can be a discussion between an agency leader and a few students who are engaged in working as volunteers with the group. This type of program will spark tremendous interest in student involvement.

The experience of schools which have held series of talks by community leaders has led to the conclusion that the moderator or principal should introduce the total program to the students at the first assembly, listing its purposes and perhaps proposing that students themselves suggest speakers through the student council.

As part of its intention to educate students to a Christian sense of concern for the society in which they live, a high school can step beyond student-centered programs and consider groups which are quite naturally connected with it. One such group is the Parent-Teacher Association. A lecture series can be the first step in the process of educating parents to a Christian view of society and a concern for its problems. Actually, another complete manual could be written to demonstrate how a religious order, through the utilization and formation of the lay faculty and various adult groups connected with a school, could concretely and realistically develop adults dedicated to a concern for the rechristianization of the urban community in which they live. At any rate, a speakers' program for the P.T.A. or other parent groups can help to make the parents of students, and indirectly the students themselves, more aware of their community.

A design of a workable program for a P.T.A. was made by a high school for boys in Charlotte, North Carolina. The school realized that apathy among parents was gradually destroying the association and the program was attempted as a means of increasing interest and attendance at meetings. After the first introductory meeting, the next three general meetings consisted of panel discussions of faculty and parents concerning the educational program at the school — its aims, nature, and problems; the religious program and the school's relationship to the Catholic community; and finally, the work of students involved in the civic community was highlighted. In this program, representatives of some of the participating agencies served on the panel. In the second semester, three meetings were given over to community leaders similar to those chosen for the student program. Informal discussions followed the panel discussions or talks.

One good resource person obtained from a local university was a member of the psychology department who discussed parent-teenage relationships. This, as could be expected, proved to be the program exciting most parental interest.

One coeducational high school in Los Angeles has made it a practice annually to sponsor a prominent national speaker as part of its Parent-Teacher assembly program and invites the general public to attend this session. It should be mentioned that the public school system's Parent-Teacher Associations often sponsor a nationally known figure in education, adolescent psychology, or some related field, to conduct workshops with parents and teachers. Perhaps the Catholic high schools' P.T.A. could cooperate financially and organizationally in setting up such a workshop in conjunction with the public schools.

A boys' school in Cincinnati set up a program with the local social work association which helped to initiate students' interest in becoming involved in community activities. The association sent staff members and competent case workers to the school to lead discussions with the students. Included in the orientation was an introduction to the local community, to the various opportunities for volunteer work available in the city, and to the concept of service in the community as a means of showing concern for people. Through the discussions, students were gradually able to clarify in their own minds exactly why they were interested in serving as volunteers in an agency's project. To be noted here is the fact that many community groups are so interested in having volunteers that they will go to great lengths to help develop and form interested students. Usually this formation will be humanitarian in nature and will lead the student to understand that he must have a real concern for people. It is only a step to show him that this concern for the human family is the way for him to exercise the command of Christ that we love one another.

Another aspect of a speakers' program is its public relations value. The mere fact that agency leaders and representatives of various institutions and groups in the city are invited to the school to speak improves the image of the school in their minds. It serves as an excellent opportunity to meet community leaders, to build up a list of persons who know the school and who would, upon a second contact, be more willing to cooperate with the school in possible programs.

Program Four

A TUTORIAL PROGRAM

A recent series of ads in major national magazines feature a picture of a bewildered-looking youngster and the head "I didn't know there were children who had never been read to." The simple kinds of personal interest involved in tutoring programs often are as valuable as the learning experience. The child who has never been read to has little motivation to learn reading for himself. Face-to-face learning with a friendly young person, himself a student, can provide the needed spark.

Tutoring programs have been organized in many schools for some years and recently have become major projects for such school clubs as junior human relations organizations, civics clubs and sodalities. Such programs can also be excellent training for chapters of the Future Teachers of America — introducing members of the club to the profession to which they aspire, with special emphasis placed upon social responsibility. The program on which this is based operated through such a high-school F.T.A. chapter in Pittsburgh, Pennsylvania.

Tutoring programs can be of many sizes and shapes, depending upon the number of high school tutors and younger children involved, the agency or group cosponsoring the project along with the high school, and the amount of time and work poured into the project.

Experience shows that tutoring programs with local Catholic and public grade schools will usually be more organized (and a little more demanding of time) than those which are sponsored by neighborhood community centers and local churches. By contacting the local Catholic schools, the public school superintendent, local neighborhood centers and local churches, the moderator of the Future Teachers of America will find prime areas needing volunteers to help set up, organize and carry through tutoring of local children.

Lines of communication differ in various schools but if the program is going to work jointly with grade schools, private and public, the principal of the high school should be brought in on the negotiations from the start. Usually discussions will take place with the principals of the grade schools and communication will have to be made and permission gotten from the superintendent of schools before the program can begin. The relationship with neighborhood centers and churches generally is not as structured and more flexibility is possible. The moderator may be able to handle the entire program without clearances from so many different persons — the principal and the neighborhood coordinator are usually enough.

The moderator should prepare an orientation program for those high school students who are going to tutor, in conjunction with the agency with which the project is undertaken. Such an orientation should include a series of lecture-discussion sessions on the area and neighborhood where the tutoring is going to take place. Previous contact with resource personnel can now be utilized in a concrete fashion. Much of the orientation can be left to them; their personal experience can communicate a sense of reality and excitement to the students. Participants must be led to see that a superiority complex is out of order if true service is to be given. A windshield survey of the area is often a good follow-up to the discussions and talks.

If the tutoring program is worked out in conjunction with a neighborhood center, it is advisable for it to be set up at the center rather than to bring small children to an unfamiliar high school situation. It is easier for the high schooler to travel across town than it is for an eight-year-old child.

After the moderator has contacted a neighborhood center or a school and has offered to help set up a tutoring program, he must, in conjunction with the center, work out a suitable outline of subjects which are going to be taught to the children. In most cases, English grammar, elementary arithmetic, and reading are the subject areas chosen. A very good instrument in regard to reading is the use of reading machines. Juniors and seniors in high school can easily enough master the simple mechanics and operation of these machines. They are very valuable and make a real contribution to the content of the tutoring program. Beyond this, children find them fascinating and can often be taught to run them themselves.

If the project takes place in a grade school, meetings with the principal, with teachers who have had these children in class and sometimes with guidance counselors should precede the actual beginning of tutoring. A more rigorous outline of study most probably will be demanded and closer supervision will be given to the tutor. During the summer months, through funds granted in the poverty program, student tutors working in the public schools can receive payment for tutoring. Ordinarily, this type of arrangement does not extend into the winter. If a tutoring program is going to be set up, however, such public programs as this might be taken into consideration. The moderator might have to answer the question: is there more value to having the students tutor in a neighborhood center for no pay than tutoring in the public school system with money serving as an added incentive? From another viewpoint, often some of the best student tutors must work during the summer. Involvement in public school tutoring on a salary basis can allow the student to participate in a worthwhile project that he couldn't otherwise afford.

If the program is to achieve some measure of success, the moderator should have conferences with the student tutor as often as possible about the effectiveness and success he is having with his students and about the effect the program is having on *him*. Such a project should develop a certain generosity in the high school student as well as social awareness and responsibility. An alert moderator can bring across the apostolic implications of a tutoring project to the student. Another helpful idea in this respect is discussion periods with all the student tutors participating. This can lead to greater insight through the sharing of common experiences.

As in other projects, the moderator must choose students whom he can rely on. In a certain sense, once contact has been made with the local organization in need of tutors and a commitment made, an obligation exists to fulfill the "contract." If students adopt the attitude that they can come and go as they please, this will not help the project but is more likely to undermine it. For this reason, it is suggested that the program be started on a modest scale. It can be begun as a pilot program which, if successful and satisfactory for both parties involved, can be augmented and further developed. Feedback from the principal of the local grade school, the coordinator of the community or neighborhood center, or the director at the local church is an essential. At first, feedback can be merely concerned with the fact that the student is consistently showing up for the program on the days assigned, or that he and the children are enjoying the work. Later, discussion can center around the quality of the tutoring performance and the actual help which the student is giving to the child. Such points can later be used in discussions and interviews with the student tutor.

Parental permission should be obtained in this as in other programs. In many instances, students indicate that they would like to work as tutors but fail to obtain parental permission. Much unpleasantness can be avoided later if clear permission has been gotten in advance.

A variant of the tutoring program, and one very attractive to high school girls, involves assistance at pre-school centers. Most cities have such centers to care for the small children of working mothers. While the work is more along the lines of supervising activities, conducting play sessions, and the like, the satisfactions in helping these little children are immense.

Program Five

AN ECUMENICAL PROGRAM

In a period in which ecumenical programs of one type or another have proliferated on all sides, Catholic schools have also begun making interdenominational contacts. These attempts have been often halting and incomplete, since the Catholic school, unlike many other church agencies, does not have an opposite number among Protestants and Jews. It more naturally turns its contacts toward the public school system, and on a professional rather than a religious basis.

Nevertheless, the Catholic school is instrumental in forming the attitudes of its students. Beyond this, its faculty are often one of the leading groups of church-related professional people in any community. Their impact and that of the school and its student body should be felt in the growing dialogue among Catholics and others. Since diocesan regulations regarding participation in ecumenical programs vary from place to place, this Action Program will necessarily generalize from several types of programs now being followed. In some areas, faculty participation in ecumenical programs is relatively free, while student participation is all but forbidden. It goes without saying that a Catholic institution can hardly enter into any program without proper authorization. This is perhaps all the more necessary in the instance of the school because of the unique image the Protestant public has of it.

The Protestant image of the Catholic school often is a curious one. It ranges from fairly sophisticated ideas to the most antagonistic. Not uncommonly the Catholic schools are seen as highly divisive in the community, or as mere propaganda centers for the Church. One of the authors recalls meeting a public-school teacher who was surprised to find that Catholic high schools taught other courses than religion!

This program is centered upon faculty participation. In this area, at this time, student contacts seldom go beyond study days and occasional cooperative projects. Faculty members, however, are in a unique situation in the community. As professional people they have a natural contact in the city. As persons staffing a religious institution (especially the religious staff themselves) they are accepted as representative Catholic spokesmen. The Catholic schools being among the most obvious Church institutions in the city, many of the public assume that the school somehow speaks for the Church. There is an obvious fallacy in this to anyone who has known the Catholic secondary school well, but correct or not, it is part of the public image projected. It seems incumbent upon the school faculty, therefore, to begin establishing contacts in the Protestant and Jewish communities. With their education and background, they are particularly suited for this, and the profit to the school and the student body are not insignificant. As faculty members form personal friendships from among the non-Catholic clergy, a newer and more meaningful kind of dialogue will develop, one that will be of great benefit to the total community.

For any ecumenical dialogue there are various guiding principles that should be observed. It must be conducted in an atmosphere of charity and mutual understanding, with respect for the diversity of views of the participants. For Catholic school teachers who in any way represent their institutions, some diocesan authorization is usually necessary. In general, the dialogue will progress best if it is a quiet affair without wide publicity. Those involved should have some notion of the social implications of interfaith discussions, and there should be an attempt, through study, to understand the basic positions of the other participants.

For the high-school faculty member, there are some added dimensions to the dialogue. Most probably, the discussions will not center upon strictly theological points, and it is not likely that it should. The aspects of greatest concern will tend to be areas of mutual interest in the community and the exploration of possible cooperation on programs and projects. This type of cooperative effort has been common for Catholic social work agencies, and it offers considerable avenues for development for the teacher.

The most obvious area of cooperation is youth work. Protestant churches conduct numbers of young peoples' programs and Sunday school activities which can be articulated with the Catholic high school in many ways. In some cities, exchanges of teachers between Sunday schools and high-school religion classes have proved interesting and valuable for students on both sides. Here the teachers have the opportunity of sharing their own ecumenical dialogues with their students, helping them to understand the viewpoints and attitudes of other groups in their community.

A second area of cooperation in social action programs, either involving students or among the teachers and others is the interfaith dialogue. Where an existing dialogue had progressed to the point at which the participants could act together to demonstrate their commitment, this has been shown particularly effective in interracial activities. A number of other types of social action programs can be undertaken on an interfaith basis. Where such things as student study days and meetings are involved, the Catholic school is often in a position to offer its facilities.

In one other Action Program in this book mention is made of interfaith retreats. This type of program, which is spreading throughout the country, provides a relaxed and truly Christian atmosphere for exploring areas of common interests and tension points in the community.

As a result of his own contacts with other churches in the community, the Catholic teacher is in a position to expand the contacts of his students. Many of the projects described elsewhere can be undertaken in an interfaith context. In many cases, profitable contacts can be made with groups of Catholic students attending public schools. Their insights into interfaith relationships can be enlightening to Catholic youngsters who have never attended public schools. Contacts with Catholic teachers employed in the public school system can add an area of cooperation that will prove of value to all concerned.

With common professional interests, they share many concerns with the Catholic high-school faculty, and are often seeking an opportunity to serve their Catholic pupils through church-related programs.

No teacher needs to be told that student interfaith dialogues will hardly be profound. They can result, however, in expanding the horizons of the participants. No one can better take leadership in this than their teachers, and no one is better equipped to guide them over misunderstandings toward greater cooperation with others of differing faiths. One presently-operating program in Norwood, Ohio is a fine example of the type of student program of continuing value. In this program, the Catholic high schools worked out an interreligious study day in cooperation with Protestant student groups (such as Hi-Y) that are organized through the public schools. What makes this something more than similar programs across the country is a program for continuing the dialogue among the students. This is accomplished by exchange visits among Protestant Sunday schools, CCD classes, and religion classes from the Catholic schools. With competent adult leaders as resource persons, this program is a valuable educational experience for all concerned.

Program Six

A RECREATION PROGRAM

Travel around any city, especially in the poorer sections, and you will see hundreds of children on the streets, playing aimlessly together in a fashion which mirrors lives already frustrated, hopeless, and severely limited. For these children, many of them not more than seven or eight years old, school itself has already become the scene of failure and the long hot summer months do nothing but reinforce the feeling that no one really cares for them and no one is interested in them. They learn at an early age that their struggle against the dismal, crushing effects of the slum is a fruitless one. They can't play a game of baseball for there is no equipment and, even if there were, no one would be around to keep "the bigger kids" off the field.

The existence of neighborhood and community centers has done something to alleviate this problem. Through the neighborhood organization, small children can find attention, games and, above all, a place to play with some type of supervision. Various indoor and outdoor projects are designed by the centers and often programs are set up to take children on trips throughout the city, on picnics, to baseball games. For problem children, the Big Brother and Big Sister programs were designed as an attempt to provide a masculine or feminine image to a boy or girl who needs this guidance and example because of the loss of a father or mother. Due to limited manpower, however, centers cannot care for all the children in a neighborhood. Recreational programs are often the dreams of a volunteer coordinator rather than the concrete existing projects they should be.

Under these conditions, school moderators who approach a community center coordinator suggesting that the two sit down to plan and outline some concrete programs for his high school club should not be surprised to find the coordinator's interest at a high pitch. Usually, it is quite easy to organize the details of a recreation program. The program will take place during certain hours on particular days of the week (often suited to when the high schooler can be there) and seasonal outdoor as well as indoor games can be planned. Model airplane building, checkers, tag — depending upon the age of the children — will be played. Often the center will not have much in the way of recreational equipment and old materials which the school no longer needs can be channelled in its direction. The school might sponsor some type of drive around Christmas for the benefit of the poor in the community. Materials and games collected from the drive could be given to the neighborhood center.

Many times, students will be able to organize and develop new types of recreation, such as day-long picnics, tours around various interest spots in the city, even arranging leagues for various sports among different community centers. Innovation and imagination can be used to good advantage.

To overcome the lack of playground facilities plaguing many centers, children can be brought to the high school for some recreational activities, especially football and basketball games. Occasionally, groups could attend the athletic functions of the school as its special guests. If such is the case, the moderator should make sure that the center is fully aware of such a program and permits it. In most cases, the center will have to arrange parental permission for such activities. At any rate, it is a good thing that the school and the neighborhood organization work together closely for the total benefit of both the children and the students involved in the program.

Teachers and moderators of school clubs are well aware of the silent portion of the student body that does not become involved in any school activity. Many of these do not even attend the athletic programs of the school. Often this group is a sizable part of the student body and it is important that some type of social formation reach them as well as other more active students. Tutorial programs, involvement in interracial activity, and CCD programs perhaps would not suit them nor would the moderators of such groups encourage their participation. A recreational program is often the type of program that appeals to these youngsters. Often students who are not members of other clubs and groups turn out to be the most consistent workers in projects of this type and often they do the best work. Recreational programs in parks and community centers can involve unlimited numbers of students who would be generous enough to give up two or three hours a week to supervise and participate in games with smaller children. Some schools have fifty to seventy students involved in recreation programs of this type.

The great value of these programs from the school's viewpoint is that it is possible to use so many students who are willing but not particularly talented. And who is to deny that they, too, need social formation?

Program Seven

THE DOMINICANETTES

The picture is so obviously unposed that it is a delight to see: an elderly woman who could be anyone's grandmother being helped to walk by a sweet-faced Negro girl with a bright smile. The note written along the side reads "Dominicanettes come in all sizes, shapes, and colors." The nun who added the caption might well have been describing the Dominicanette program itself — its activities are as varied as the simple needs of the poor and the ill. To list some of them is to describe one of the most sophisticated action programs for high school girls. The Dominicanette program is directed by the Dominican Sisters of the Sick Poor. Although other congregations of sisters have developed groups of helpers along the same lines, the Dominican Sisters' program is based on some twenty years of experience.

The particular apostolate of the Sisters is the care of the sick poor in their homes. The Dominicanettes began simply as a means of recruiting volunteer assistance to help with the many needs that did not require professional nursing training, such as visiting the elderly, preparing defective children for first communion, handling summer outings for patients, and other projects. As the program has developed, spiritual development for each participating girl has been added, including a monthly holy hour and semiannual days of recollection. The results of this combined program of apostolic involvement and spiritual development are not surprising. Many have discovered religious vocations as nursing sisters, and one sister superior writes:

> Once they become aware of the need to serve, it sticks to them. Many are now teaching sisters, with a real and living awareness of the needs of their fellow man.

In addition, numbers of girls have been inspired to enter careers such as public health nursing where their abilities to serve can be put to full use.

The recruitment of girls into the program is either through the contacts of the Dominicanettes themselves, or through programs conducted in Catholic girls' schools. These are arranged with school authorities and often conducted entirely by the Dominicanettes. After expressing an interest, each girl is interviewed to evaluate her abilities to serve and her idea of what service is. Some are never able to give direct care to the sick but can make other contributions to the program.

The personal interview begins a period of orientation. The girls are told what types of work are available, and are trained to do those things which they are capable of handling. The completion of a course in home nursing is required before a girl may visit the sick with a sister and assist in giving home care. While a complete job cannot be done in the fourteen-hour training program, the girls can be introduced to basic techniques and get some idea of the kind of service needed.

As mentioned above, many types of work are undertaken by the Dominicanettes. The sisters' experience, however, has shown that all the girls do better work when they visit the sick poor with one of the sisters making her regular rounds. For this reason, every girl is assigned to a professional nursing sister if the girl is to help out in the patients' homes. This constant contact and supervision assures that the work done by the girls is well done, and that the needs of the patient are being properly met.

Most of the girls in the Dominicanette program will be found doing all the simple but vital tasks of a homemaker. Beds need to be made, sick babies watched while a mother shops, an elderly bedridden man needs to be shaved, an old woman needs the comfort of someone to talk to: the works of mercy come alive in the persons of Christ's poor. But there are many other kinds of work. One Puerto Rican family learned English from a Dominicanette, for example. Entertainment, religious instruction for children — the activities read on like a litany of charity. The casual remark of a teenager that "it's a real treat for an old lady to get her hair fixed," reveals more than the simple fact she has discovered. She has learned as well to rejoice in the happiness of others.

Twice a month the girls taking part in the program hold meetings at which they plan all their activities. Included in each of these meetings is a discussion on the apostolate, helping to bring out the girls' attitudes toward their work. The sisters have found that the girls are better reached by their peers than if one of the sisters herself tried to explain the "why" of many situations that they encounter. This initiative and responsibility are encouraged whenever possible. In one city the Dominicanettes wrote a pamphlet to describe their work to other students. They wrote it themselves because they objected that the sisters had written it in too-fancy language!

One of the natural contacts that Catholic girls' schools have in setting up apostolic experiences for their students is social welfare programs directed by sisters. These programs offer the great advantage of professional supervision under trained personnel who are familiar with the Catholic school system and sympathetic with the desire of teaching sisters to find suitable apostolic outlets for high-school students.

Program Eight

JUNIOR ACHIEVEMENT

The Junior Achievement Program is so widespread among both public and Catholic schools that it is included here more for completeness than because there is any need to bring it to the attention of teachers and administrators. It is the most successful program using a format by which an outside agency provides complete direction of students. It also is the best program in wide use for introducing students to the business community and the free enterprise system.

Simply enough, the Junior Achievement program makes it possible for groups of students to establish a small business, either in manufacturing or by providing services, in order to understand the American business system. Junior Achievement will recruit interested students each year, and inform them about the program. It then puts them in contact with cooperating business firms in the immediate area, which serve as sponsors. Students are not grouped by school or age.

A group of students who have an idea, usually connected with the type of work done by the sponsoring firm, will come together to form a corporation to produce their product or provide their service. The usual legal incorporation procedures for a corporation will be followed. Stock will then have to be sold by the students involved, and the capital realized from stock sales will constitute the working capital. If the venture loses money, the stockholders will not receive all their money back — the sponsoring company does not "bail out" failures, so incentives to succeed are high.

The types of work undertaken under Junior Achievement supervision include every imaginable business activity. Manufacturing of small, saleable items is common. One will find many others, however, such as a company which conducted a survey of teenage purchasing habits, and sold the results to record shops, clothing stores, and other interested outlets. The sponsoring company was a prominent data-processing firm. A radio station might sponsor a group to put on a regular program, for which the teenagers solicit advertising, and which they plan and direct. At least one high school has contemplated having its yearbook run as a Junior Achievement project, independent of both school moderators and the school budget!

The experience can be an invaluable one for many high-school boys and girls. It is planned specifically as a learning experience, and after a set number of months, the corporation must be liquidated, and the stockholders paid back their investments, plus or minus any profits or losses. The direction given throughout the process by businessmen gives the student an insight into business processes that he might not otherwise get. In addition, he will be thrown in general contact with the sponsoring corporation, its operations and activities.

The Junior Achievement system has proven itself so successful, in fact, that one wonders why it has not been applied to some other aspects of the school program. Any large Catholic high school has many extracurricular activities that are entrusted to the care of the faculty. How often a complex activity is thrust upon some teacher who is ill-equipped to handle it and already overworked.

Even a small city offers a number of outlets for this common problem. A number of professional groups are quite willing to sponsor career-oriented groups, such as a school newspaper, and provide an enthusiastic and cooperative moderator. One small school, pressed to provide a drivers' training program, countered by enlisting the volunteer help of the Fathers' Club to provide supervising drivers. The Dominicanettes, described in Program Seven, are an excellent example of the use of a competent outside group to direct apostolic experiences for students. If such programs can be undertaken, there is little doubt that many others could be supervised in cooperation with community agencies and talented volunteers. It only takes a willingness to think in imaginative terms.

Program Nine

MEETING THE DROP-OUT PROBLEM

Among the social problems that directly affect the school are those that undermine student motivation to remain in school. The lure of jobs and immediate pocket money is very tempting to a boy from a poor family, even though the job may be a dead end with little or no opportunity for advancement. If the student has had a poor record in school as well, the temptation to quit at the legal school-leaving age may be almost impossible to resist. This is an in-school type of social problem, but one with implications for the entire community.

If there has been any kind of drop-out pattern stemming from economic causes, the school guidance director should be able to pinpoint potential drop-outs. The need is for a program within the school, involving various available services, to motivate the youngsters to finish their high-school educations. The program cannot be theoretical if it is to be successful, and it usually must begin well before the legal school-leaving age.

One program used successfully in a number of public schools has been the establishment of a Careers Club. In this action program the use of cooperating agencies is being included as well, to show some of the possibilities along these lines. There are several advantages to structuring such a program within a traditional school organization. Much of the social stigma attached to being a "special case" is removed, especially if various students join who are probably not potential drop-outs. One of the difficulties of the potential drop-out is that he rarely takes part in school activities of any kind. Some of this sense of estrangement can be overcome by a group that he finds practical and attractive, and which caters to his natural interests. There must be enough of the latter so that the youngsters will feel that his immediate interests are being served, while his long-term interests are being protected.

The student members of the Careers Club can be recruited in the usual manner, so that the group is an open one, but the real potential drop-outs will probably not heed a general call to join another new school organization. Much of their recruitment will have to come at first through personal contact, both from interested teachers and guidance personnel. It will be important that the group not be limited to potential drop-outs only. After the program has been well started, there should be some recruitment by the students themselves, as the attractive elements of the program get to be known by others.

The easiest and fastest way of satisfying the students' immediate concerns is to have a part-time job program as part of the club. In a sense, this "defangs" the major allure of dropping out of school by putting some money in their hands at once. This should not be looked down upon — it is a real need for the youngster who cannot keep up socially with his fellows, cannot dress decently, and perhaps must depend upon school or parish assistance to stay in school. Accepting assistance is always somewhat degrading, and the feeling of making his own way is a powerful motivating force for a boy or girl.

Job placement can be organized through the school guidance program, and it provides a good excuse for some valuable guidance interviews with the type of student who usually resists traditional guidance. If the guidance personnel are inexperienced in vocational guidance (often the case in Catholic schools) or overworked (usually the case in Catholic schools), they can get assistance from the local office of the state employment agency. An agency representative will provide information on how to proceed and usually offer help in getting lists of available part-time jobs in the area. In some cases they may help with actual placement. Very often the local Chamber of Commerce will give its good offices toward opening part-time opportunities with local businesses.

In this regard, it should be mentioned that Catholic schools are eligible to cooperate in the programs of the Office of Economic Opportunity (Poverty Program), which provide for paying students at the minimum wage to perform needed work, the money presumably helping them to remain in school. In this way some Catholic school systems have acquired teachers' aides for elementary schools with overburdened classes, student office assistants, laboratory assistants for science teachers in the high school, and library clerks. Student aid cannot be used to replace any existing jobs, but this rarely presents any difficulty, as Catholic schools usually are in need of extra assistance. Various other programs for youth operated under the Office for Economic Opportunity provide the same type of part-time jobs in public services such as libraries, public schools, recreational centers, and the like.

Eligibility is determined by need, and opportunities are available for both boys and girls (especially in hospital work). Usually administered through the public school system, students from Catholic schools are equally eligible if they fulfill the financial need requirements. As paid assistants these students are often for the first time brought into contact with various public and volunteer agencies. Some agencies take such student aids with a specific purpose of motivating them toward finishing school and entering public service careers. Some East Coast police departments direct internship programs of this type, combining work after school and on Saturdays with orientation toward entering police and public safety work after graduation.

Once the Careers Club has recruited students and begun a job placement program for those desiring it, the club usually sets up a series of talks and demonstrations on job opportunities, with strong emphasis upon the value of continued education for getting or holding a position of any kind. The advantages of the graduate over the drop-out are stressed. Business groups, social agencies, and others often are happy to provide interesting down-to-earth speakers for school groups.

A big problem lies in making the transfer in the mind of the student, so that he or she sees the necessary connection between finishing high school and later success in life. Boys especially may be particularly impressed to find that even the armed forces recruiters will emphasize the importance of having a high-school diploma for advancement in the services. Making the connection between job opportunities and academic work is not too easy a thing for a student who has a record of repeated failure or who finds classes dull and uninspiring. A good means of meeting this need is to introduce a tutoring program for students in need of help. It would be admirable if the classroom teachers could do this for all those who need help, but there are obvious limits to their time and energies. Teachers who have tried tutoring programs where the work was done by the better students in the high school itself often find that many youngsters sign up for help, but few can be found to do the tutoring. Even at best, this system does not work too well. There is one community agency that can be asked to help, however, and which can provide competent tutors. By contacting local colleges and universities for volunteer tutors, a teacher will often be able to obtain assistance from prospective teachers who are only too anxious to work with students.

A tutoring program using college education students has many advantages. The students from the college are eager, young enough to empathize with teenagers, and relatively competent. At the same time, the high school itself is providing them with a real opportunity for professional growth, and the teacher from the high school will be able to perform a highly valuable service for his profession. The advantages for the poorer student being tutored lie in increased learning and higher motivation.

When someone takes a personal interest in a poor student, perhaps for the first time since entering high school, the best conditions are set up for success in academic work. The teacher, of course, should be ready to help the tutors! At first, they will often be uncomfortable in their new roles and a little frightened of their responsibility.

The desired aim of lowering the drop-out rate is the goal of the program, and by using available civic groups and agencies the work of the school can be much extended. At the same time, valuable contacts and areas of cooperation have been established for future developments and other programs.

Program Ten

A NEIGHBORHOOD YOUTH CORPS

It has been mentioned elsewhere that the main concern and involvement of the school in social action programs is with students' social formation. The general norm is that the school should not be undertaking project-oriented programs. Project direction is the task of various social agencies; student supervision and formation is the task of the school. This Action Program gives an account of an exception to this proposition, in which a small high school undertook a program under a grant from the Office of Economic Opportunity (The Poverty Program), and directed a program based upon student participation.

The scene was Victoria, Texas, a small western city with a coinstitutional Catholic high school. The school is racially integrated, but the largest minority group is made up of Mexican-Americans. To meet a need for recreational areas in an older section of the city, the school Sodality undertook an interesting neighborhood development program. One student living in the area noted that a vacant block lay unused in the heart of the oldest neighborhood, and the idea of the development of a small part was discussed. Investigation showed that the property was owned by the city. After a preliminary investigation it was decided to use the property for recreational facilities for the people of the area if possible. A student commented in the school paper:

> The aim of the Queen City Project sponsored by [the] School and Sodality is to get American citizens of all races, occupations, religions and creeds working together for the common good of all through economic betterment.
>
> The whole program is considered a practical education in social justice which aims at breaking down the cycle of poverty and of dispelling prejudices that give many of our students the feeling that "all" those who are poor or of a different racial background are lazy and don't want to improve themselves economically.

Important to initiating the project was taking a survey to determine the real recreational needs and the feelings of the people of the area involved. This wise precaution helps to ground any such program in reality, and helps to avoid having the students and teachers impose their own notions of what is needed in a neighborhood. (A copy of the survey questions is included at the end of this case study.) The survey consisted of visits and interviews with all the parents in the area by teams of students. About 129 families were interviewed, and the city's mayor and a local district judge were involved as consultants.

With the survey results in hand the school moderators and students visited city hall to see the mayor and also to present the findings and an outline of the project to the city council. The school was able to present the city officials with an officially organized set-up which provided financing by negotiating an agreement with the Poverty Program. Under the terms of the grant, which was officially received by the diocese as grantee, several of the faculty were named in charge of a Neighborhood Youth Corps project. The principal of the boys' high school was appointed director, and students working on the project received $1.25 per hour. The city was asked to supply tools, equipment, guidance, and a sum of money to cover the expenses of creating the park. The land also had to be allocated by the city as part of its contribution.

With city cooperation assured the project went ahead. Students from several schools in the area, including residents of the neighborhood itself, were hired by the Neighborhood Youth Corps to work on the project. Since the program aimed at getting area residents involved there was concern to enlist youngsters from the neighborhood being benefitted. The money received by the students was to provide an increment, minimal though it might be, to the incomes of families in poverty areas. Paid workers ranged from the students who manned hoes and shovels up through the student project assistant to the faculty coordinator of the program. The neighborhood being served occupied twenty-one city blocks, the area of the survey.

Eligibility was largely determined by federal regulations. Applicants must be citizens or permanent residents of the United States, between the ages of sixteen and twenty-one, unemployed or working less than twenty hours per week. In addition, the student must be a member of a family whose total income fell below the limits in the following table:

Allowed Annual Family Income for Eligibility

Family Size	Non-Farm	Farm
2 persons	$1990	$1400
3 persons	2440	1710
4 persons	3130	2200
5 persons	3685	2580
6 persons	4135	2900
7 persons or more	5090	3560

The work started with cleaning up the vacant lot, which hadn't been touched in years. Fence posts were made from poles donated by a local utility company, and these were set in the ground around the entire block to prevent vehicles from entering the play areas. Paint for the project was donated by local businessmen, a truck was provided by the city, and trees to beautify the park area were given by a private donor. The design for the park, drawn up by students, was accepted by the city administration.

Part of the students' experience included attending an urban renewal seminar and the state convention of the NAACP, where they discussed the role of religious institutions in civil rights work. As a result of the meetings the students met urban renewal officials, local Negro leaders, and important city officials such as the city housing inspector, all of whose cooperation they needed in further projects.

These contacts helped to give a broader perspective to the students' experience, but the program also included a built-in guidance and evaluation program. Each student participated weekly in one and one-half hours of group guidance, and had a fifteen-minute personal interview each week, all in addition to on-the-job supervision.

The success of the program is indicated in a remark of the mayor that he has thirty-two other park areas where student help would be appreciated. The group has petitioned the city council for approval to set up a youth center in an abandoned house near the neighborhood park. Several other unsightly spots near the school have been cleared up, and there is evidence of a growing pride in the appearance of the older neighborhoods.

The students have had a tremendous learning experience. It is an open-ended experience, since every day seems to afford new opportunities for expanding activities. The students have had a chance for down-to-earth dealings with public officials as well. They have dealt with the diocesan poverty office and the federal government. They have met outstanding cooperation as well as frustration and misunderstanding and much red tape. It is hoped as well that they have met Christ in their neighbor as they learned to bear witness to their faith.

The Survey Questionnaire Results

1. How many boys and girls do you have living in your house between the ages of 5 years and 18 years?

129 families in survey	*Family with children between 5 and 18*	*Children*	
		boys	*girls*
	70 families (54%)	101	88

2. How many days a week do any of your children use the present park facilities?
   Families not using parks at present time 90%

3. Do you think that the park area needs improvement?
   125 families answering Yes 78% *No* 9% *Undecided* 13%

4. Would your children use this area if it were improved?
   103 families answering Yes 63% *No* 29% *Undecided* 8%

5. What type of playground equipment would your children most probably use?

Number of   swings, 61   basketball court, 24
requests   slides, 43   merry-go-round, 34
              baseball, 17   monkey-bars, 13
              miscellaneous, 30

6. What are the occupations of the men in your household? (The purpose of this question was to locate residents with skills which would be helpful in park improvements.)

7. Would anyone in your family be willing to help improve the park area?
   119 families answering *Yes* 41% *No* 40% *Undecided* 19%

8. Classify the family living in this residence.

129 families in survey	*Negro Families*	*Latin-American Families*	*Other Families*
	45%	39%	16%

Program Eleven

A MULTIPLE PROJECT PROGRAM

So far, we have been dealing with specific individual projects that have been worked out in school situations. What of a total program? It is not enough to say simply that a school must study its situation and determine what areas it can and should deal with. When a broad program is developed, there are two possible approaches. Either a central coordination of activities is used (as in the program for a small girls' academy given elsewhere in this handbook), or an *ad hoc* kind of approach will develop. Individual faculty members and student organizations may take up projects of their own. The advantage of such a variety of projects is the flexibility given to students who prefer one type of work over another. Unless coordination is razor sharp, however, many projects will become bogged down and gradually die out.

This case study is from an urban community in the "mission territory" of the Southland where two percent of the city is Catholic. A Catholic high school for boys with an enrollment of 170 and a faculty of eleven (six religious and five laymen) has launched a series of projects designed to acquaint the student body with the city they live in — its institutions, people and problems — and to form these students in an attitude of responsibility to that society. They hope to form a deeper apostolic commitment in as many students as possible. The teachers are expected to conduct five classes a day, moderate several activities each, and serve as guidance counselors to the student body. In many respects — mainly its size — the school does not fit the pattern of many Catholic high schools in the country. It serves, however, as an example of what a well-coordinated multi-project program can do even though the school has limitations of personnel and facilities.

The program described here is now in its third year of operation. Originally, an emphasis was laid upon research aspects and only later did students become involved in projects centering the inner-city. Both aspects are now coordinated simultaneously.

Through the use of newspapers, students plotted on maps the names and location of the city's industrial, educational, religious, governmental, recreational and cultural centers and outlined major ethnic concentrations, religious groupings, and areas of heavy crime activity. Contacts were made with local resource organizations and attendance at meetings of local groups became a valuable introduction for students interested in getting involved in activities in the urban community. Most of this activity was organized and developed by the Sodality and the civics club.

A lecture-discussion series was developed at the school, consisting of invited leaders of various agencies and groups who spoke to the students on the work of their agencies, some of their problems, and relationships to the general community. A discussion period usually followed. Resource persons from the Chamber of

Commerce, the local Board of Education, the police department, the city manager's office, and from the cultural arts center were some of the participants in last year's program. It is important that not only competent persons in their own right be chosen to give such talks but that those chosen be good speakers if the program is to get off the ground and hold the interest of the students. The worst thing that can happen to such a program is the appearance of a poor speaker, a long hot afternoon, hard chairs and the threat of detention for the person who gives in to the human tendency to distraction in such situations. Vital and stimulating speakers are a must.

The civics club, with the cooperation of the Sodality and the student council, organized a project in union with the local anti-poverty agency which utilized students who volunteered to work in one of three neighborhood centers and a Protestant church. The students were engaged in such diverse activities as serving as big brothers to small kids who had no fathers, supervising recreational activities for neighborhood children, and serving as tutors to children needing extra help in school work. They drove clients of the poverty agency to shop, to see their doctors, to visit the hospital, and the like. Many poor children of the city had never seen a world that is not grimy and filthy, and the students took them out of their neighborhoods to see their own city and its museums, parks and swimming pools.

The poverty agency itself gave a thorough orientation program to participating students on three successive afternoons after school. The orientation sessions were required by the agency and consisted of a series of talks on the background and scope of the poverty war in the city. There were group discussions concerning the work of the neighborhood centers, and a discussion in which student attitudes on the poor were brought out. The students who thought they were great white knights coming to the aid of defenseless, poverty-stricken people, were distinctly shocked. Lastly, a windshield tour of the area was taken and a short discussion was held to show reactions to the tour.

Parental reaction was neutral to favorable. The agency demanded that parents sign a paper absolving the agency of responsibility for accidents, etc.

It should be mentioned that constant effort must be made to recruit the right students, as characterized by a certain degree of social awareness, responsibility and maturity. If arrangements are made, dates set, and the students do not come for their programs, the project is in danger of collapsing before it starts. Perseverance of those involved is a requirement of extreme importance. A significant aspect of this program was its continuation over the summer months to the satisfaction of both the poverty agency and school authorities.

Frequently, the Optimist Clubs or similar organizations sponsor an annual youth appreciation day which can serve as an excellent jumping-off point for civic involvement if utilized imaginatively. In the city being described here, these feature mock sessions of the city council. In two successive years, the student representatives from the local Catholic high school have raised issues — pornographic literature and teenage drinking

— which prompted the establishment of special teenage committees to examine the issues in question. City elders were taken aback a little when the teenage council discussed such relevant topics and proposed concrete suggestions instead of merely taking over the microphones for polite speeches. A valuable aspect of this project was that it led to increasing connections between the public schools and the Catholic school on the student level.

In many cities, youth councils are being organized representing each of the area high schools and youth from lower socio-economic levels who often are dropouts. A school can make important contributions to such a council, and influence its decisions and orientation, if students representing the high school are imaginative in their thinking. If programs are organized in the school which communicate the decisions of the city-wide council and serve as a forum for suggestions and for discussion of issues, a great deal of social formation can take place in the school. Logically, such a program could be organized as part of the civics or sociology courses of the social studies curriculum, as was done in the school under discussion. If this is not feasible, special clubs could be organized for the purpose, although the full spectrum of student opinion and reaction will be missed.

Another project was volunteer work with the local chapter of the American Red Cross. If parental approval is given and the student is fifteen or over, he can help out by serving as an assistant in hospitals, often involved in manual work, but frequently in tasks which involve direct contact with patients. The Red Cross conducts a six-hour orientation program before the student volunteer is permitted to participate. This type of work admittedly is more suitable and attractive for girls but boys will participate if the idea of service is put to them in an appealing manner.

If acceptable to the local bishop, various types of ecumenical programs can be worked out, similar to the one described in another part of this section. Since this area is a sensitive one in this city, one-day discussion programs were worked out with the cooperation of the public school and some local group such as the National Conference of Christians and Jews. Such modest programs have initiated a process which could lead to greater ventures in the area. The organization for such day-long seminars usually was initiated by the National Conference with local schools invited to participate. Follow-up programs are the responsibility of the local school. The National Conference supplies the speakers and often will contact local Catholic schools for resource personnel to lead discussions on some aspects of the Catholic religion, since these programs usually attempt to organize various discussion groups dealing with the three major religions. An excellent opportunity for cooperating with a civic organization is provided in this case.

Aside from the ongoing programs mentioned above, various projects have been taken on which last one or two days, and two of these should be especially mentioned: civil rights demonstrations and involvement in supporting political candidates for elective office. Both are extremely touchy areas and should be approached with caution.

Students occasionally will seek to "do something" in regard to civil rights, especially if their religion or social studies teachers have been stressing the topic in class. Often, the urge for involvement leads to a desire to be involved in some type of demonstration or march rather than a deeper commitment to bettering human relations in a neighborhood by working in a neighborhood center or at some similar activity. If the involvement is sponsored by any school club or organization — such as the Sodality or civics club — a careful examination of the demonstration and its aims and methods, the groups sponsoring it, should be made by school authorities. To avoid unpleasantness later, the moderator of the club should demand that those involved obtain their parents' permission for such a venture.

If the school is convinced of its mission to form its students in an attitude of Christian responsibility to society, it would do well to permit involvement where proper safeguards are maintained. Many times, the very appearance of students from a Catholic high school can be apostolic. In this Southern city, the Church's image in the Negro community is largely determined by what the Catholic high school does in regard to civil rights since parish witness on this topic is relatively minimal. The hiring practices of the school (two teachers are Negro), the number of Negroes enrolled in the school (twenty percent), and student activity in the arena of civil rights contribute in large measure to the image that the Negro community has of the Catholic church.

In another respect, students involved in such activity are forced to reflect back upon what they are doing and why they are doing it. An alert moderator can seize upon this situation and use it to develop an apostolic commitment on the part of the student.

Another equally sensitive area is cooperating with political candidates running for elective office. The school maintained a completely neutral policy in this regard, allowing student clubs to assist anyone who asked for their help. In recent elections, the civics club organized groups of students to pass out bumper stickers and the like for a candidate running for the state house of representatives and the civics club, in union with a student combo and the poster club, organized entertainment mixed with political campaigning for a state senator. .In both cases, the candidates themselves approached the groups and asked for their assistance. The school as such was not identified with the candidates and no problems developed. As an aside, both candidates won handily and one led his ticket.

Although all of these programs are taking place in a small school of 170 students and other projects are being planned, the significance of this operation lies in the variety of programs and projects undertaken. The school's program has benefited through this variety. The school does not look upon all of these activities in themselves as apostolic, but conceives of the boys' formation by the religious and lay faculty as inculcating apostolic values in the students.

Program Twelve

A PROGRAM FOR A
SMALL GIRLS' ACADEMY

It is always easier, it seems, to envisage a community relations program involving student activities in terms of a large coeducational or all-boys' high school. This excellent example of a program for a small girls' school comes from Cincinnati, Ohio. The school in question is directed by a diocesan-based order of nuns, and has less than four hundred students in grades seven to twelve. The program is multi-faceted, involving faculty and administration on a voluntary basis, and students as a required part of their education.

The principal of the school, who also teaches a senior course in social studies, is herself very active in community affairs. She serves on the board of the neighborhood community council, and has been elected as secretary and board member of a coordinating agency which approves all Poverty Program applications for the city, a metropolitan area of over a million population. Through her own work in the city as well as her professional status, she has established and maintained contacts with most of the important public agencies in the area, as well as with the public school system. Through an Office of Economic Opportunity work-study program, the academy has several part-time student clerks.

The school which this dynamic nun directs is private and draws students from many parishes throughout the eastern half of Cincinnati. Located in a changing neighborhood which sister's neighborhood council has helped to stabilize into an integrated and slowly reviving community, the school shares the concern of neighborhood leaders for an improved situation and an end to deterioration. Most of the girls from the academy either enter college after graduation or enter professional schools for careers such as nursing. A large Catholic high school for boys is located within easy walking distance, as is a diocesan girls' college. There are friendly relations among the three, but few areas of cooperation have been explored. The same order of sisters directs the local parish elementary school.

As the student program described below took form over the past several years, various members of the faculty, both religious and lay, began to take active part in community affairs themselves. A few of the sisters have undertaken a hospital visitation program at a large public hospital for the poor. This and other developments along the same line are encouraged by the principal and the mother superior, but are left to the initiative of the faculty members.

Beginning with the notion of developing practical experience for girls seeking information on future careers, sister set up a Prep-Careers Program to enable the students to become involved with agencies and institutions in fields in which they expressed interest. This has grown until today all senior girls must accept an assignment in some type of civic or social activity as part of the required senior course in civics-sociology. The requirement extends only to a single semester, but continuing work is encouraged. The dimensions of such a program are very different from an after-school type of operation with volunteers. A small amount of school time is allowed by having early dismissal one day a week, and great care must be taken in placing the students in situations in which they can contribute meaningfully. Strict adherence to attendance and punctuality is insisted upon, but little difficulty has been experienced in this regard.

In general the girls are pleased with the program, and many are openly enthusiastic. They have transmitted some of this enthusiasm to other schools through their natural contacts with friends in other Catholic high schools. In short, they "talk it up." The agencies and institutions who have used the girls as assistants are equally pleased. A few teachers who reluctantly accepted teachers' aides at first now compete keenly to get an assistant each year. The adult supervision has generally proved satisfactory, and sister places girls only where competent professional supervision is available. By having the program as an extension of a class, there is opportunity for group discussion and evaluation. Sister is particularly pleased with this laboratory aspect of the program. Parental objections, perhaps surprisingly, have been few, and there is general support of the program from this direction. There are no assignments, however, which require a girl to work with an agency or institution at night.

The areas of involvement themselves are relatively

simple. The three major fields are hospital work, elementary schools, and some teaching. For the first few years the girls were placed as teachers' aides only in Catholic schools, but this has recently been expanded to include a slum public school serving one of the poorest areas of the city. The request for help in this case came from the public-school principal, whose daughter attended the academy. Further expansion will depend upon the number of girls available. The teaching engaged in by the girls is confined to released-time Confraternity of Christian Doctrine classes for small children from public schools. The girls must have some training to participate in CCD work.

Work in hospitals also requires some training, and the hospital itself usually provides this as part of its own volunteers program. As mentioned elsewhere, the Red Cross often conducts orientation programs for volunteers who wish to help in this type of work. Since most hospitals have well-organized volunteer programs, the integration of teenage students is not difficult. Competent and sympathetic supervision is usually assured. The work done is similar to that done by "candy-stripers" and other younger volunteers. Where agencies provided or required a uniform for the girls, the academy allowed them to wear this on the day they did their volunteer work, in lieu of the regular school uniform. Inevitable comments and conversation among the underclass girls were the natural result.

Given enough students to meet ever-increasing demands, a girls' school has many other avenues to explore. Tutoring programs for underprivileged children are well known in many cities. Work with orphans and retarded children can be a rewarding experience for many young women. One special program treated elsewhere deserves mention as well — the Dominicanettes. For many years the Dominican Sisters of the Sick Poor, who nurse the poor in their homes, have organized groups of high school girls to help them in their tasks. The tasks may be simple, but they add the dignity of Christian love to the lives of both the needy and those who serve them.

Program Thirteen

A DIOCESAN COORDINATING CENTER

Although the program described here is a highly sophisticated one that has been in operation over twenty years, it represents a coordinated program for a large city that would be possible in many urban centers with a number of Catholic schools. The program described here is not limited to high-school youth, but extends to young adults and others. The primary focus, however, is with teenagers either from Catholic or public schools. The great advantage of a center such as this is its ability to provide services and programs that might not be within the limits of possibility for a single school. A center allows centralized direction (by no means always popular) as well as centralized facilities. As programs operating through the schools become more highly developed, however, a central staff and headquarters can provide services that might otherwise become burdensome, such as contract negotiations with public agencies and foundations when seeking grants.

This center operates in Minneapolis, Minnesota, the seat of a diocese with a well-developed Catholic school system with a number of high schools. A diocesan priest is director, and several lay staff members assist him. They use a converted residence with sleeping facilities for about forty persons, a chapel, dining room, ballroom, and offices, recreation space, consultation rooms, and the like. The center is located near the heart of town, convenient to public transportation. The sleeping areas include separate facilities so that both boys and girls can be accommodated simultaneously at weekend programs.

The purpose of the center can be phrased as a concern for Christian commitment. Whatever is done, either at the residence or in one of its activities held elsewhere, is geared to developing a sense of Christian commitment in the young people involved. This is brought out and strengthened in teenagers by special weekend retreats called seminars. From these a number of other activities spin off into parish groups, high-school groups, and social action programs. Because it serves a wide area, the center works through a variety of programming devices that are designed to suit a number of age groups and particular needs.

The weekend seminars gather together about twenty boys and twenty girls who follow a program of conferences, discussions, common recreation, and prayer not dissimilar to many newer retreat schedules for teenagers. The schedule runs from Friday evening to Sunday noon. There is emphasis on the daily Mass, which involves full participation, often a very new experience for students. The theme of the seminars is that of Christian love, stressing the great truth that God's love of us is a personal thing that calls for a personal response on our part.

The discussions and conferences take up such topics as student problems, sex and chastity, the Mass as community action, and the social commitment of the Christian. The total program strongly emphasizes the aspect of community spirit. There is no rule of silence during the day, so the students will have a chance to continue lively discussions and get to know one another. There is a period of cleaning up and housework, and two social hours. Various methods are used to help each teenager to get to know the names of the other participants early in the program.

These seminar programs, not unlike the outlines and themes used by the Retreats of the Christian Community given by the teams of the Movement for a Better World, could be offered in any conventional retreat house. The advantage of having this type of retreat, however, is the opportunity for follow-through. The center not only provides a general means of follow-through, but has two specific levels of commitment for teenagers with built-in follow-up programs. One level involves joining a CONTACT group in the local parish or school, the second involves joining what is known as the CORPS, a leadership group.

The CONTACT groups make up the diocesan Catholic youth apostolic organization. This is a high-school group which operates somewhat along the lines of the Young Christian Students, with spiritual and apostolic action part of its regular meetings. At the school level it is largely led by the CORPS members, with the assistance of adult moderators from the faculty. On the parish level the CONTACT groups are led by CORPS members who are moderated by adult members of the parish who are selected by the pastor. They are usually married couples who are trained by the center. The parish CONTACT groups meet in private homes.

The second level of commitment, the CORPS, numbers about thirty percent of those who are members of CONTACT. Involvement in the CORPS means that the student is willing and anxious to give more of his time and energy than the ordinary teenager to the task of the christianization of society. CORPS members attend a special meeting at the center each month in small groups of about fifteen. During the month they also meet with their adult moderators and also with the action members of the CONTACT group to which they belong. In reality they are the leadership of CONTACT on the parish and high-school level. Their leadership may be formal or not, but in fact they are the leaven of the entire program.

One notable aspect of this program should be pointed out before going on into a further discussion of other activities of the center. This is the relatively smooth articulation between parish and high school. There can be a certain interchanging of membership, and the formation of both students and moderators comes from the same source. The continuing problems that some high schools experience in establishing any type of rapport with the parishes on the apostolic involvement of teenagers is thus brought a long way toward solution. The parish receives the added benefit of building up a nucleus of apostolic men and women who have through the CONTACT program, and of trained leaders who have served as moderators for the groups.

Besides the seminars, weekend retreats of a more conventional type are given periodically. Joined to these retreat activities are evenings of recollection aimed specifically at high-school students attending public schools. These offer an opportunity for bringing these young people into parish CONTACT groups as well as providing them with the retreat opportunity itself. These "Twilight Retreats" are a means of acquainting public-school students with the center, and can begin contacts with other Catholic teenagers who attend Catholic high schools.

One interesting project has been the Junior Peace Corps, a summer program. One summer, seventy-five boys and girls spent several weeks working in a variety of activities on an Indian reservation in the Dakotas. They did everything from tutoring and supervising recreational programs to showing Indian girls how to use makeup and fix their hair. All the activities were an expression of the works of mercy in some fashion or other. The impact was highly successful. This type of ambitious program would be extremely difficult for a single school to organize, but a center can do it with much greater ease.

A number of programs operate from the center for the benefit of young adults who are out of school. While they do not directly concern the high-school student, they have a particular value in that they provide a continuation program, something that apostolic endeavors in the high school cannot normally undertake. By using the center, which most of the active teenagers know already, there is a smoother change-over to out-of-school apostolic activities.

Among the other programs being regularly undertaken mention should be made of leadership training sessions for Catholic public-school teachers who are interested in taking part in center activities; meetings with parents who work with the center; interracial home visiting programs; lecture series; marriage preparation programs; and participation in an interfaith camp each winter, in which well over a hundred teenagers of various denominations come together. One further activity is of special value: the moderators of high-school apostolic groups meet regularly at the center to compare notes, arrange areas of cooperation, and to coordinate programs.

The emphasis throughout the center's manifold activity is on spiritual, apostolic, and social action formation. Even the recreational programs for young adults are distinctly Christian in tone. The center staff has not found it necessary to have an athletic program in order to attract youngsters. The athletic facilities amount to two ping-pong tables and two pool tables in the basement — a disquieting vision to those who feel that a great deal of time must be devoted to athletic programs in order to be effective with adolescents.

Inevitably, finances for such an ambitious undertaking are a major concern. The center budget runs about $140,000 per year, most of it covered from fees charged for various programs held at the center. The remaining forty percent of the budget comes from occasional benefits held throughout the year, donations and an annual grant of $24,000 from the diocese.

The advantages of a center program of this type are quite clear for a large city, and are economically feasible. Even a smaller city, however, usually has some type of facility that can be programmed to accomplish many of the same ends. There are numerous cases of retreat centers and recreation centers which have integrated apostolic programs of one kind or another into their basic programs. The point for the high school is the availability of a Catholic resource center for coordination and integration of a multitude of activities that go beyond the abilities of an individual school.

Program Fourteen

THE PLACE OF THE SCHOOL SODALITY

What's happening here in our action programs is an interesting historical development. Although civic involvement has its basis in fundamental social philosophy, its recent development in Catholic schools can be traced to definite events. The widespread Catholic Action movement of the thirties gave practical impetus to school people to get their students consciously involved in the social movements within the school and later within the community. Their goal was to prepare students for future roles in the adult Catholic Action structures. The exigencies of practical week-to-week school life caused these efforts to evolve into special school activities concerned with the religious growth of the members and with initiating just about any meaningful student activities. For a while the emphasis was on the former with the gospel inquiry of the YCS (Young Christian Students organization) and the spiritual development discussion of the Sodality dominating the weekly meeting. Both groups were in the habit of referring to themselves as apostolic groups because of their basic aim of Christianizing the world; their effectiveness in this area depended largely on the originality of the leaders and moderators.

The direction in the Church soon tended more and more to a universal involvement of the laity. Through the fifties the tight structures of Catholic Action loosened. By the time of Vatican Two it was generally accepted that all Christians should be involved in improving the world. In fact secular movements such as the Peace Corps, the poverty movement, protest movement, the growing popularity of the teaching profession, and even the lyrics of many popular songs indicate a national trend toward meaningful social involvement. The programs, case studies, and very existence of this book give evidence that the Catholic school has become very concerned with giving each student practical apostolic training.

Have Sodality and YCS put themselves out of business? The correspondence of a network of sodality moderators in the mid-west showed a typical development of thought. We have succeeded, they told one another, in making the entire school into a sodality. Almost every student is to some extent consciously involving himself in the betterment of society. Our religion courses, capitalizing on the experiences of the students, have become forums of practical spiritual development. The student council organizes all activities and provides a day-to-day leadership workshop. Guidance counselors and activity moderators check on the development of individuals; the faculty guides the complete movement. We can no longer speak of sodality moderators and sodality cells. Every faculty member is a moderator and every student activity a cell. Although our total organization needs much development, we have achieved a certain perfection of form. We have no more need of the school sodality — our school itself is an apostolic organization.

There is no doubt that a certain perfection of form has been reached in such schools, and yet the argument fails to consider the most outstanding trait of the Sodality and YCS, the trait that enabled it to effect the present situation and the trait that makes it even currently indispensable. The Sodality or YCS is uniquely capable of forming intensely Christian leaders — and these are even more crucial in our apostolically mobile school.

Let us consider this basic trait of Sodality-YCS before treating the structure of the organization. The school's apostolic group should play a major role in bringing about the entire program proposed in this book. Although the faculty runs the involvement program, its whole tenor has to be one of student interest. Students who become interested in the works convince other students. The recruitment of new workers must be done, at least in part, by other students, largely in order to be certain that the values in the system will be internalized. A big problem in any mass educational endeavor is that students will feel themselves victims of the faculty's will; they'll put up with classes and do the minimum work, blind to any values. Most teachers have seen students turned off in even excellent courses because of an apathy grown from unwilling compliance with other people's ideas. The more the students participate in the school out of desire the more they are fully educated. The whole question amounts to recruitment. The more the student is recruited to being a cause of an activity, the more he is educated. Teachers have always recruited students with a special interest in a subject: they have recruited students for special helpers, for project workers, for future teachers, and for injecting a special enthusiasm into the class. The student who spends his afternoons on a physics project, especially if he is well respected by the other students, strengthens the class's attitude in the course. The fact is of extreme importance in involvement programs. The students must be there because they want to be and they will want to be if it is their own project, their own idea. The educator is at his best when he is providing professional service to the students instead of prodding them on or playing truant officer. The recruitment of the workers then is best done by students themselves or by a faculty member with a facility for getting his recruits to internalize the project and carry on the work of recruitment themselves. The organization for recruitment would be the Sodality-YCS or the student council. In a school beginning an involvement program, the practical situation would determine whether student council or Sodality-YCS would take the job. Sodality-YCS is generally already founded for this type of work. The interest of the student council would depend on a number of factors, but it should be involved somehow, at least eventually. If the members of Sodality-YCS are not the type for the job perhaps a new group should be organized, for the second recruitment job demands highly motivated and well respected operators.

When the workers are assembled and the job begun, the work of recruitment is by no means finished. Even when every student in the school is involved, the biggest recruitment job is still to be done — recruitment to the deeper values of the work. Teenagers, and for that matter human beings in general, are notorious for losing interest in anything. Basic facts like family fights and coffee breaks evidence man's need for renewal. The most glamorous assistance programs, such as caring for the unvisited on a children's home's visiting day, have proven to become a drag to even the most generous high school students. For most activities the boredom rate is even higher. Sodality-YCS members have the continuing task of recruiting fellow students to interest in the activities. A bulk of the meeting time, in fact, would be spent in rediscovering the values in the projects and planning how to pass these insights on.

The natural development of the sodalist or YCS member involved in such a task would take him deeper and deeper into the meaning of the action program. From these insights he receives the impetus and ability for recruitment to the values involved in the projects. Here the religious motivation behind the entire program comes to the fore. Even though in most action programs, the actual job itself is religious in a way that working math problems is not, the educator still has as a prime motive the forming of the student's mind — not just his mental ability to perform the function, but his internalization of the reasons, the meanings, the concept of reality involved. Wisdom is above facility; the teacher hopes for a student who can perform a function and has a free, open mentality that enables him to do much more than just perform the function. An educator knows the student's social formation is not complete because his present actions help society and he knows the student's religious formation is not complete just because he is currently practicing spiritual or corporal works of mercy.

Many aspects of the formation program must be organized to lead the student to a conscious realization of just what he is doing, a practical awareness of the human values to be stressed and a deepening feel for the religious meaning of his work. The religion course should concern itself with these goals and the moderator of each activity should have a regular interview program to work at them. But for two reasons the Sodality-YCS must do much of the job. First, they can bring realization from within; their insights come right from the front lines. Billy Graham's crusades, the Better World Retreat, the Sing Out meetings have all evidenced the strong effect of the testimonial on teenagers. The sophomore in tutoring who tells what it meant to him when his eight-year-old student said "I missed you on Christmas" is communicating human values most realistically to his fellow students. True, the organization of a works program should structure formation through testimony; yet alert Sodality-YCS members can be constantly at work at this task — especially in the informal situations that count the most. A strong group of well respected apostles can dominate the students' attitude toward a project, exercising a constant guard against the development of negative attitudes, and causing a growth of the most Christian mentality.

Second, the sodalist or YCS member by taking this task on himself is receiving the best possible training. Even if the services of student leaders were not so crucial, the special training of the more insightful would still be a most important activity. Those involved in bringing the mind of Christ to their fellow students are enriched with the best of the entire program — they internalize most really the values and they learn Christian leadership through practice. The faculty, by running much of the program through Sodality-YCS, is training the students who will themselves one day run the program and run the civic community. The school that graduates young men and women motivated to be the unselfish directors of the civic community contributes to society in a most powerful way.

Since we are now speaking of Sodality, we should keep in mind that it is a Christian community formed by a public act of consecration to Mary made by its members, who live this consecration by internal development of the Sodality community, recruitment to the Sodality, performing the spiritual and corporal works of mercy, and working in the institutional apostolate (the action of a smaller group on the organizations, practices, and attitudes of a larger community). Sodality is an adult organization. The high school (and college) sodality is actually a formational group, forming some of its members to eventual consecration in the adult sodality and some to an intense living of Christianity in other ways. The tradition of the sodality has always allowed for degrees of consecration and so the high school sodalists can, with a probationary status, be members. But the sodalists should be aware that sodality itself is for adults; such an awareness gives them a proper perspective on the nature of their work and prepares them for adult membership. Adult sodalists should be in contact with the high school members and ideally should have a part in their training.

To keep a high school sodality vital and true to its

nature, the moderator should be particular about membership, limiting the consecration to those students who are effectively involved in the work and are religiously mature enough to make a meaningful act of consecration to Mary. A student active in the school program who wishes to join sodality should be prepared by a series of interviews before coming to meetings as an aspirant. Many sodalities have the members vote on the final acceptance of new members. There must be some form of screening, because sodality has to continually be on guard to keep from becoming a religious bull session; hangers-on and soured members prevent the group from living its life and performing its service. On the other hand, sodality must not be an exclusive clique. The solution to both these problems is to demand very much of the members and to accept as members anyone who lives up to these demands. Teenagers like a strong challenge and those who will make good sodalists will appreciate the demands. Of course, we expect that those who *wish* they were generous enough to join will talk down the organization. Moderators should not be discouraged at having a small sodality. Experience has shown that any lowering of standards to get numbers soon makes the sodality no sodality at all and then the deadening "Sodality never does anything" attitude develops. Few high school students have the insight to keep alive in a group that does nothing but give life and depth to other organizations. The generous, religiously minded student not yet capable of being a sodalist should join one of the regular involvement programs in the school.

Only the rare sophomore is mature and experienced

enough to be in the high school sodality. But a definite plan should be in operation in the freshman and sophomore divisions to develop the students who will join sodality in the junior year.

How should this development be undertaken among the underclassmen? Certainly it could well begin by programs of involvement that already exist inside the school, as well as outside it. An alert teacher or counselor will discover a few students among his workers or in his activity or class who are more generous than the rest and capable of seeing more deeply into the real needs of other people. These students he will gradually draw aside and work with more intensely in private talks or in group discussions — both formal and informal. He will attempt to make them aware of Christ living in them and in other people, of the bond that unites all Christians in Christ and of the place of Mary in the whole life and work of Christ. He will, after some time, present them with the possibility of founding or of joining a group which endeavors to dedicate itself wholeheartedly to the Christian life and the Christian apostolate under the direction of Mary. Of course, the eventual acceptance of the sodality as an organic reality in the student's life is made more possible by the fact that he has already begun to live the Christian life more fully and has actually taken on more and more of the attitudes of a sodalist without realizing it.

We have discussed at some length apostolic involvement among high school students and the role of YCS and Sodality in furthering this involvement. Undoubtedly, time spent encouraging this involvement and especially developing YCS and Sodality takes one into difficult and sometimes disheartening waters — but those who have ventured in have found the efforts worthwhile. It would certainly be a hope of the editors of this book that it might lead a few others to take the plunge.

Program Fifteen

FACULTY ORIENTATION

Shortly before the opening of the school year, many schools hold a faculty orientation for new teachers, so that they might be familiar with school policies and procedures. A significant addition can be made to this type of program by including an orientation to the community which the school serves. Teachers should come away from the programs not only with enough background to begin working with their students intelligently, but also with an understanding of the school-community relationship that presently exists. School policies on participation of students and faculty in community action programs should be outlined, as well as a description of channels of authority within the school for developing and supervising such programs.

The guiding principle involved is the recognition of the fact that the school has definite obligations not only to the student, but also to his or her parents, the community and the Church, which sponsors the school. These four relationships determine the execution of the mission of the school. All teachers, including those who are not interested in active participation in any type of community action program, should be encouraged to see their assignment as a contribution to the total mission of the school. This they primarily discharge by their professional contribution, since the first community obligation of any school is a basic academic preparation of the students.

Some of the orientation might well be spread throughout the school year, and occupy some of the time ordinarily devoted to staff meetings and/or departmental meetings. This gives the opportunity of bringing the experienced faculty up-to-date on recent developments in the community. In describing aspects of this program, in use in a number of secondary schools, orientation to school policies and programs is omitted as something that is common practice and well understood already.

Each teacher should be supplied with a list of such ready information as may be needed from time to time during the academic year. This would include such matters as arrangements with the public school system or other public agencies for pupil services: school psychologists, vocational programs, social work programs, visiting nurses and the like. Names of contacts, if teachers are expected to handle referrals themselves, and types of services available, should all be clearly indicated.

Members of the administration and faculty, with perhaps some staff members from local agencies, might give several orientation lectures to acquaint the teachers with characteristics of the city itself, with a view toward understanding the backgrounds of the youngsters who make up the student body. An analysis of pupil characteristics, and a general overview of the neighborhoods sending students to the school are the essential elements. Some generalizations about the family structure, ethnic backgrounds, and general economy of the area will prove useful in understanding the students from the viewpoint of the community from which they come.

If time is available, it is highly desirable to see the neighborhoods themselves. In one school outside Philadelphia this is done by having new faculty visit each parish elementary school that sends a significant number of students to the school. At each visit, the principal and pastor meet the faculty members and briefly discuss the neighborhood they serve, the type of Catholic families that live there, general cultural background, etc. The teachers come away from such meetings with a clearer notion of what is expected of the school. Any special problems arising out of social conditions can be brought out at these meetings. It is not uncommon for this to be joined to a general meeting of all elementary and secondary school teachers from the high-school district (if districting is followed), at which common interests and problems can be opened up for discussion.

Some type of continuing follow-through seems to be necessary if full profit is to come from the orientation program. Many schools presently are restudying their curriculum and total mission in terms of the renewal in the Church, and the departmental discussions along these lines can add considerably to the awakening of community consciousness among the faculty. One area of responsibility that is directly related to the academic is professional activity, and the follow-through program should serve to familiarize the newer staff members with the professional associations in the area. One of the first areas of community participation for any teacher should be in educational associations, especially those established for teachers in various subject-matter fields. These groups bring to the Catholic teacher the added value of a regular professional contact with colleagues from the public school system. Organizing opportunities for professional growth is an often-neglected activity of both school administration and departments, and has important civic values.

In a situation where separate boys' and girls' high schools serve roughly the same area, another aspect of follow-through might be the establishment of a regular liaison with the school's opposite number for cooperative action on social questions. An annual meeting of the staffs of the two schools might add a new dimension to both faculties' insights into the secondary schools' operation in the area.

Similar articulation programs might well be planned with the principals and staffs of area public schools, local clergy, members of area neighborhoods councils, and other similar groups with a natural interest in the development of the district which the school is serving.

Evaluation of the orientation program is a valuable way of keeping it from bogging down into just another series of meetings. A committee of competent faculty might ask the newer staff members for their suggestions for improvement in areas which they felt needed greater stress.

Program Sixteen

FORMING LAY TEACHERS
TO SOCIAL ACTION

Amid growing rumors that by the end of the 1960's lay teachers will outnumber religious in Catholic secondary and elementary schools, many religious orders and diocesan authorities are faced with the necessity of rethinking and evaluating their approach to their "lay assistants." For years, lay teachers have been considered as substitutes for the religious faculty, migrant workers until enough religious could be recruited and trained to staff high schools.

This attitude on the part of the religious faculty, coupled with exclusion from policy-making decisions, has led to a spirit of separation from the goals of the school on the part of the lay teacher. Often, religious and lay faculty have served side by side without having the same goals for their students. If no real effort has been made to translate clichés about the aim and purposes of Christian education into concrete programs of formation (aside from religious courses), such a communication gap has appeared to do damage to the school's program of apostolic formation. Now religious orders have realized that they must integrate the lay teacher into the formation of true apostolic Christians for more than practical reasons. In many areas, lay teachers are ideally suited to handle such formation. This, perhaps, is why so much is being written about "lay teacher formation" — how a religious order prepares lay teachers to assist in the formation of students for the apostolate. The entire faculty should, in various ways and on many levels, be convinced of the need to form socially aware Christian students. The lay teacher will probably feel more at home and be more competent in some of these areas, although he might be more limited than the religious in terms of time available to work with students due to family considerations.

Essentially, the purpose of any lay teacher formation program should be to communicate to them, through formal and informal means, the religious society's approach (philosophy) to education. In the most generalized form, this approach is to form educated students who are realizing what it is to be a Christian in today's world and who are preparing for active participation in the Church's apostolate.

Presupposing that the religious society understands its mission in the high school and is attempting to make its goals practical to the high school student, much lay teacher formation can take place in faculty meetings, special discussions on the subject, and through the individual contact of religious with lay teachers. Many schools have organized retreats for their lay teachers which are designed to initiate the lay teacher to the philosophy of education of the religious society, to begin the development of a real dedication to the work of the society in the lay teacher and to stress that the relationship of the teacher and student must not end with the instruction given by one to the other but must continue with the development of Christian values. This retreat program has now reached the stage in which the lay teachers of entire provinces are invited. Many schools follow this program with days of recollection during the year in which ideas and views concerning the lay teacher's role in the school are freely discussed and talked through.

This program has led to a clarification of ideas on the part of many lay teachers and in fact during one retreat, resolutions were passed which committed the lay teachers to participate in the setting up of a Lay Teacher Formation Program at the individual schools from which they came. In some high schools a professional sodality of lay teachers has been formed — lay teachers of this group have begun to moderate various student clubs involved in social action and to moderate student sodality groups.

This type of approach presumes that the religious faculty is itself conscious of its role in apostolic formation, and that most of the lay faculty are not. Such is rarely the case, but the unhappy fact is that young Catholic college graduates are seldom apostolic-minded, and some type of in-service formation in the school is needed. There is no reason why the retreats, conferences and discussions cannot be together, and cannot be directed by both lay and religious faculty.

Even when retreats, special faculty meetings, and days of recollection have helped lay teachers see that the mission of the school is not just instruction and academic formation, a problem remains in identifying, recruiting and forming lay teachers (and many religious) specifically to moderate and organize social action student groups. Certain teachers — religious and lay — will just not want to work along these lines and perhaps the greatest criteria for choosing a lay teacher as a moderator is his manifest interest and desire to moderate a group. Other characteristics would include his or her ability to work with boys or girls, his teaching competency — a good teacher and somewhat out-going — his or her acceptance of the concept of apostolic formation and a willingness to spend the time and effort necessary for involvement in a program. Personal contact on the part of the religious faculty is the greatest and most effective means to identify these characteristics in a lay teacher and to recruit him into a program. Sometimes, the principal can make suggestions along these lines, excluding administrative pressure, of course. The faculty chaplain is of great benefit through talks given at days of recollection and through personal contact.

Through the use of workshops, special meetings and retreats, conferences and the like, a program might be worked out whereupon those interested in learning more about possibilities of moderating a social action group could do so. Included in this formation program would be an outline of the existing school-community relationship, reasons for what is being done and its aims, general information about the civic community (the use of community resource personnel would make this more effective) and areas of possible involvement. A welcome feature would be discussion in which those religious and lay faculty members previously involved would comment and give practical insights gained from experience. The ability of religious to communicate to the laymen their real desire to see them work along with the religious in the apostolate is perhaps one of the most important aspects of recruiting and developing lay teachers in this area. If the religious permits the lay teacher to feel that he is involving himself in something which is purely in the domain of the religious, the program might as well be forgotten and the hours spent in some other work. In the final analysis, the lay teacher's experiences as a moderator will help him overcome the problems inherent in working in a program of social formation. The hardest work, perhaps, will have already been accomplished: he is involved.

Program Seventeen
FORMING RELIGIOUS TO SOCIAL ACTION

An important element in any social action program in a high school is prepared teachers who can set up and supervise programs with a certain amount of expertise. Although the program described here does not involve high-school students, the entire question of formation of younger religious is of such great moment that it could hardly be excluded. Many seminaries and houses and formation have begun programs of this sort, and some are more sophisticated than others, but the one chosen for this section has special characteristics which are illustrative of the common experiences of most religious orders. Organizationally, the program is rather superior to most. In practice, it is less than ideal. One participant referred to it, with a touch of sarcasm, as "a program that almost works." Be this as it may, "programs that almost work" are far more typical of the present state of apostolic formation of young religious than those that are resounding successes.

It would be incorrect to say that the only motivation for establishing this program has been to prepare teachers to undertake social action programs in the high schools. A major consideration has been the wider aspects of formation, seeking and experimenting with newer approaches that will effectively develop the interests of the so-called "New Breed" now so dominant among younger members of all congregations. If it is tentative in approach, so are they. If its approach is highly experimental, so is their own toward their future apostolic work. Its heuristic nature is its main characteristic. The problems that have arisen in the program have largely been due to lack of competent administration; there simply are not enough experienced religious to handle this type of formation program adequately. Therefore, it is noticeable that community resource persons are relied upon rather heavily. In addition, the initiative and even much of the ordinary operation of the program is in the hands of the students themselves.

This program is that of a large scholasticate (over two hundred) of temporary professed religious men of college age. Almost all are preparing for teaching careers, and carrying full-time courses in various fields of studies at a large Catholic university to which the scholasticate is affiliated. The freshman class takes all its classes at the scholasticate in a rather restricted atmosphere; the other students pursue almost all their courses at the university. The course of study is from three to four years, depending upon previous college studies, the needs of the congregation, and the ability of various students to take accelerated programs. No credit is given for the social action program, and it must be fitted into the free time of the scholastics. Various religious, either on the staff of the scholasticate or of the university, advise and/or moderate different aspects of the program.

The basic theoretic part of the program is handled

through a weekly lecture/seminar program that runs for the entire length of the student's stay in the scholasticate. It embraces all students, including working Brothers being prepared in the trades. Although the program varies somewhat from year to year, depending upon the current staff, it generally is as follows:

Freshman: Problems of Society and the Church in the World

Sophomore: Theology of the Church and the Catholic Church in the United States

Junior: The Civic Community, its Institutions and Agencies

Senior: Theology of the Apostolate and Techniques of the Apostolate

The junior program is largely conducted by a series of community resource persons who lecture and hold discussions on the organization of the civic community, community structure and the locus of power, and the work of community social agencies. About thirty speakers are invited in annually, most of them professional people with wide experience in their particular fields. The senior program emphasizes practical aspects of apostolic work with high-school students, concentrating on apostolic formation of teen-agers. In addition, the seniors have a one-semester credit course in theology on the social teachings of the Church.

Because various visiting lecturers are used, the program suffers somewhat from lack of consistency. At the same time the advantages of having people from the field outweighs this. Experienced moderators of high-school groups participate as lecturers in the senior program. In general, the program is well received, although it has frankly proved difficult to demand much outside reading because of the heavy demands of the regular academic program.

The sophomores begin their introduction to the practical apostolate by taking part in retreat programs for high-school seniors, conducted at a retreat house on the property. They lead discussions with the students and assist in other ways. Many sophomores also prepare themselves during this year for the basic certificate enabling them to teach in the program of the Confraternity of Christian Doctrine. This program is directed by a nun who is a specialist in this area.

In the junior year, various of the scholastics begin to become involved in outside programs. By the senior year all of the young men will have had some experience. The senior program is voluntary, but placement and assignments are given each year to almost all seniors, including working Brothers. They may request what type of work they would like to do.

To suit the varied interests of the scholastics and their varied competence, a number of different programs have been undertaken. In fact, many requests for help have been turned down simply through lack of available manpower, although an occasional program was refused because it was too difficult or would be too time-consuming. Whenever possible, out of consideration for the academic responsibilities of the scholastics, programs were chosen that required only one evening a week in addition to the weekly seminar.

Seven participation and three educational programs

have operated in the given year being described here. (There are some variations from year to year.) The educational programs, described below, are also voluntary.

By far the largest number of scholastics participated in CCD instruction in various parishes in the city. With the obvious need of the parishes for this type of help, it would have been improper to ignore the requests that came in. Several students have taught for two or three years in these programs, under the supervision of the person in charge in each parish. The regular CCD syllabus for public school children was followed. In a few cases, the pastors encouraged further work among the teenage students in the parish, such as organizing picnics, hootenannies and youth programs.

Smaller groups worked with the local Catholic orphanage and with a program for retarded children, under the supervision of the professional staff. They helped with arts and crafts, worked on recreation programs, and helped prepare the retarded for first Holy Communion. Interestingly enough, these two groups seemed to have the greatest *esprit de corps,* and continued their program through the summers.

At the request of a local Protestant seminary, a group of interested scholastics participated in the direction of a weekly religious television program, under the moderatorship of a member of the seminary staff. Although much of the leadership in this project came from the Protestant seminarians, who were several years older than the college-age religious, the scholastics contributed considerably to the programs, which were highly successful.

This proved a valuable ecumenical project which developed many other areas of contact with local Protestant seminaries of other denominations. As the first year progressed, nuns from a local juniorate of sisters began to take part. This juniorate is also affiliated with the same Catholic university.

A fifth program involved providing assistance to the city's children's detention home. In this case, the scholastics gave some short courses to the boys in the home, and also helped in the recreation and crafts program. One former U. S. Navy veteran, for example, gave a series of talks on opportunities in the services. There were similar programs with several Boys' Clubs.

Several young religious were assigned as teachers' aides in a public junior high school in a suburban area, working under classroom teachers who proved very cooperative and enthusiastic about working with the young men. Assistance was given in the areas of natural science and language arts.

The last program involved several scholastics in work at a Catholic-sponsored community center in the city. They assisted, under the direction of the staff, in programs with children and teenagers, and also helped with the recruitment of student volunteers from the university. They spent some time helping organize neighborhood teenagers to fix up the center and improve its facilities.

The three educational programs were different in character from the participation programs. The first of these was a series of T.A.P. tours conducted by social workers from local agencies. These Truth About

Poverty tours operated by having a religious assigned to
a particular social worker for a day, accompanying her
on her rounds and trying to get an insight into the problems of the poor. At the end of the day the scholastics
would get together to swap experiences and share what
they had seen. The tours opened a few eyes to the realities of the problems being discussed in the weekly
sessions.

The second educational program was a longer and
more highly sophisticated one. A group of students
formed a club to undertake a community study project
and to acquaint themselves with the structure of the
community more thoroughly than the weekly lectures
did. Much of the leadership for the weekly lecture series
came from this group, which often chose the speakers
for the lectures and handled details of the program. One
group spent a summer formulating a program for the
continuation of the community study by later classes.

The last of the educational programs was the most
experimental, and was only indirectly related to the total
program. It was a program in sensitivity training, directed
by three trained group dynamics leaders, none of them
Catholics. This program was arranged by several interested scholastics, and was taken by about thirty seniors.
It consisted of three three-hour weekly sessions, running
for three weeks in the summer. Although the time was
much too short, each of the three groups ended rather
enthusiastic about the experience. The three groups
operated on a T-group basis,* with a few other group
activities. The broad concern in this program was the
development of a sense of community among the par-

ticipants, and a growth in sensitivity toward interpersonal relations. There is neither space here, nor is this the proper place, to discuss this program in detail. Due to the transfer of one of the leading trainers the following year, the program has been repeated for a smaller group only. It remains, however, as an area which deserves further exploration, if only as a general formational method for younger religious.

This brief account gives some detail on a not atypical program for a house of formation. Others like it in one way or another have been set up in scholasticates and seminaries around the country. In this particular program, weaknesses appeared in evaluation, which was not well enough structured and was seldom as profitable as it might have been. There were the usual failures, but this is not to be attributed to the program so much as to the human condition. Inexperienced CCD teachers experienced discipline problems among their young charges, for example, and some scholastics found that they were not up to handling some of the tasks that fell to their lot. Nevertheless, the growing experience of each added year brings the program closer to the ideal situation that is envisaged.

————

*T-groups are essentially unstructured sessions, without formal leadership or agendas. On this see Spencer Klaw, "Two Weeks in a T-Group," *Fortune* LXIV, #2 (August, 1961), 114.

Program Eighteen

AN EXPERIMENT IN NEIGHBORHOOD PENETRATION

One of the interesting developments among religious over the past two years has been the proliferation of small communities of lay religious living in housing developments, changing neighborhoods, and slums. Some of these, quite naturally enough, are groups of religious engaged in social work or specializing in teaching the culturally disadvantaged. Besides these communities, however, there are others made up of graduate students or teachers in traditional schools. In most cases, these religious are living as they are and where they are out of concern for the poor. Without being viewed by the people as social workers, they hope to associate with them as neighbors, and to make themselves available to them on this basis. These attempts to approach a neighborhood community with the witness of religious community lived among the people are too new to evaluate, and it is not within the scope of this book to do so. What is described here is one such experiment involving the faculty of a Catholic high school.

The faculty members in this situation are four religious Brothers teaching in a large central Catholic high school for boys. The school draws students from many neighborhoods, and there is a cross-section of socio-economic groups represented. For some time there has been interest in social action among both the religious and lay faculty. One lay teacher began a tutoring program for children from disadvantaged homes, the first such program of its type in the city. For several years, one of the Brothers on the faculty was a board member of the local Catholic interracial council, and various interracial projects have been developed. There is a loyal alumni, and the public image of the school is a good one.

The school itself is located on the fringes of the city's business district, in a poor Negro area that is slowly being consumed by highway projects and business development. The local parish is across the street from the high school, and cooperates in a number of ways. It has no elementary school, and very few Catholic families. Its former school building is used by various groups, and the church has been a center for many *cursillistas* from the city. The religious community, of about forty men, lives in a community residence adjacent to the school, and is almost completely out of touch with the neighborhood.

For over a year, four of the religious faculty have lived in another part of the city, in a small house leased and furnished by a group of laymen who have assisted several other projects among the poor of the city. It is a simple residence, no different from the rest of the homes of the area. This particular neighborhood, almost entirely Negro, is served by a national parish that does not consider it its mission to relate to the neighborhood. A Catholic community center under lay direction serves the neighborhood with a number of programs for people of all ages. Volunteers from Protestant as well as Catholic churches of the city help with the programs. The neighborhood itself, a poor one, usually looses any potential educated leadership, as Negroes who attain any status in the community — teachers, businessmen, etc. — invariably leave for other, better Negro enclaves in the city.

The Brothers in the residence began simply by getting to know their neighbors and becoming known by them. They have been relatively well received. One Negro leader from the city, a former resident of the area, expressed the opinion that the Brothers would find less racial prejudice against their presence than reluctance to accept them because they were teachers and professional people. This has not turned out to be clear, if it has happened. The Brothers have kept their full assignments at the high school, going to school each day by bus until they were able to afford purchasing a used car.

The problem is the amorphous nature of the apostolate in such a situation. Religious especially, and teachers in Catholic schools in general, have always had a well-defined apostolic work. Institutionalized as it is, the Catholic high school provides specialized means with clear professional standards by which performance could be judged. Even with this, however, every teacher knows how unsure of final results the faculty always is. What then of an apostolate that eschews formal work, that consists largely of the simple witness of community life in a neighborhood where community does not exist? At best, it takes an act of great faith to find any "results" in the usual sense. The religious must ask himself what being a good neighbor demands of him. How does he contribute to the growth of a spirit of cooperation so that neighborhood development may begin? These unanswered (and perhaps unanswerable) questions underline the heuristic nature of the situation.

At the end of their first year of residence in the area, the Brothers found themselves in a highly tense situation. The progressive deterioration of the neighborhood suddenly changed into a precipitate slide toward violence. When a series of small riots and looting began throughout the neighborhood, the city as a whole was shocked. The aftermath of the "time of troubles" was a community-wide period of soul searching. In the Negro ghetto this took the form of a series of grassroots meetings culminating in a lengthy report to the city commission, drawn up by residents of the disturbed area.

The religious living in the area had in this situation a clear opportunity for community cooperation. They joined the spontaneous grassroots committees that sprang up, and have remained active since this time. What is significant here is the level of activity. These men are not professional social workers nor are they engaged in this type of work. Their community participation takes place, as does that of their neighbors, after a full day's work.

There is a tendency to regard this type of experimental form of community life as meaningful only in relating the religious community and the school to the poor and underprivileged. Such a community does provide the school with a contact in the Negro ghetto from which student projects can develop. At the same time, the

Catholic high school must relate itself to a total community, and unless it serves a poor neighborhood exclusively, as many parochial grade schools do, it needs to relate itself to many neighborhoods. Perhaps what is needed is the atomization of some large religious communities into small groups scattered about a city or district, in order to see if this technique is meaningful on a larger scale. The same Negro leader mentioned above expressed the opinion that this community would have been better established in a middle-class Negro ghetto. His feeling was that the Negro professional and businessman lacked social consciousness, and the Brothers might have approached these people as equals, and could have done much to turn them toward their responsibilities to the community at large, and the underprivileged Negro community in particular. Be this as it may, we know little of the impact of a community of religious living as real neighbors in a middle-class neighborhood, even though there are many such communities. Some further experimentation is needed here also. The active religious or lay teacher in a poor neighborhood can easily emerge as a community leader if he or she is accepted. To be accepted merely as an equal is a dimension not yet much explored, as most religious communities live in, but not of, our middle-class neighborhoods. The level of participation needs to be raised, and it is difficult to see how this can be done without further experimentation along the lines given here.

Program Nineteen

THE MISSION SCHOOL:
TWO AFRICAN CASE STUDIES

In both the rural and urban areas of Africa the Church has concentrated too much on turning out a Catholic who went to Mass on Sunday and who received the Sacraments occasionally. We might say that the missionary was too concerned only with the Christian religion, with proselytizing, and with turning out Christians who concentrated on personal sanctification almost to the neglect of their neighbors. As a result the Christians were not concerned eough with the welfare of the people and with their social and economic development. This is a vital issue, for if we are not deeply concerned with people, then we can almost never get the people vitally interested in religion. The first step of the missionary as well as the Christian must be to interest themselves deeply in the welfare of the people.

To interest ourselves in the people we must have a strong conviction of the great importance of the economic side of life in the establishment and in the maintenance of Christianity. The Church cannot expect to have success with her missionary work in a rural community if most of the people are farming according to primitive methods (which means, because of the population explosion, that the community lacks food.) The missionary and the Church must first solve the problem of enabling these masses of people to live according to a standard of living fit for a human being and of making these human masses *human*. This issue cannot be emphasized too strongly because all of us, whether in the missions or even in our own country, will be looked upon with a bit of suspicion if we are not concerned with human beings first. This is a giant task for all of us because so little emphasis has been given in the past on the need to possess a deep social consciousness. We have not been trained primarily to serve society and its peoples.

This is one important quality — the need for a social conscience — that we must pass on to our students. Our students have a key role in working at the socio-economic problems of the developing countries in Africa. Even as students, they can begin to realize that they have a mission to serve society and to provide the masses with the basic material needs of a human being — food, clothing, education, shelter, water, health, etc. Our students must be made to see that these things are their concern and that these are their fields and their work because important basic moral principles are involved in these socio-economic problems.

There has been entirely too much talk in the missions about making converts. There has been far too little talk of solving the basic problems of why the new nations in Africa are not developing. In our schools, whether in the rural or urban areas of Africa, one of our prime responsibilities should be the development of the social consciousness of our students; it should be our aim to make them dynamic apostles of socio-economic development of the masses and to mold and shape them so that they possess the conviction that their role lies in serving their society. In this case study we shall try to show how this can be done first of all in a secondary school in a rural community and then secondly in an urban community in Africa. Whether in an urban or rural secondary school, the school administration must realize the importance of specialized Catholic Action groups in involving the whole school in social and economic development projects.

Specialized Catholic Action

Here in Africa many of the secondary schools are tied in with the Young Christian Students (Y.C.S.) Movement which is the specialized Catholic Action movement on a national level. This is important, for a movement gives a sense of national purpose, conducts national meetings, holds seminars involving secondary-school students from all over the country, and acts as a clearing house for ideas and materials.

Specialized Catholic Action groups provide the leadership to involve the entire student body in socio-economic projects. These specialized Catholic Action groups in the school should be small; no group should consist of more than ten members. Since this movement provides the leadership in the school, it should be an elite movement that affects the mass of students. Each member in such a group should possess strong, natural leadership qualities. From the viewpoint of intensive training, it is essential to work with a small group possessed with leadership ability. Lastly, a strong warning: the effectiveness of such groups will be determined as they help the students and the community. It must not be a group that is concerned only with its own development or ends up by being a mere discussion group. This must be an *action* group bent on service to society.

The Apostolate in the Rural Area

The rural high school in this case is surrounded by a rural community of about 10,000 people. The population is very dense and is engaged almost exclusively in agriculture, mostly primitive, although quite a bit of coffee is grown now. The secondary school is situated in the middle of a large number of villages which are joined together, forming the town.

A small sodality group of eight members from the Fourth Form was first started (this is the senior form in the school). For some reason or other, this group developed very rapidly; perhaps it was the private meetings with each member of the group which occurred at least twice monthly. Within six months this group had decided to embark on an intensive apostolate.

The group realized that they and the rest of the fourth formers had passed through the school without ever becoming involved with the problems of the local community and with the problems of the masses. It began to crystallize in their minds that they could do something for the peasant community of poor, illiterate farmers living off a few acres of land. They saw that because they had been privileged to go to school they could provide the local leadership necessary to activate the people and to initiate schemes that would help the people's development. Because they were of the people they knew the people's needs, the people's desires and aspirations.

As a first project, the group decided that they wanted to carry out an adult literacy program. This could be one of the greatest means to help this illiterate community. It is indeed one of the steps toward uplifting a rural community. Two sodalists who were put in charge of the entire program approached the African District Officer to find out his reaction to the project. He reacted very favorably and agreed to talk about the project with the three headmen in the villages. Another sodalist, in the meantime, was assigned to see the parish priest who eventually gave his wholehearted support to the project. Several weeks later the two sodalists returned to the District Officer to find out the reactions of his talks with the headmen. He reported to them that the headmen were enthusiastic about the project and that they would arrange for a group of sodalists to talk to the people in the different villages. Meetings were held in the three villages by various sodalists and the people decided several things at these meetings: 1) the people wanted to learn English; 2) many of them wanted to learn to write their own native language; 3) most of them wanted to learn simple arithmetic; and 4) the program would operate three afternoons a week from four to six in the early evening.

The next step was to find the teachers. At this point a large number of students were utilized and this helped to involve the entire student body in the project. The sodalists approached the students in Form Four and practically every one of them answered the call. The problem of textbooks was solved through money received from generous people in the States, although the people who attended the course were charged a nominal fee amounting to about fifteen cents in American money. At the height of the program three schools enrolled 350 people (too many of them children) taught by fourteen Class Four students. The moderator's main work in the program was to supervise the teachers who naturally required a great deal of attention, especially in the beginning.

Resulting from the adult literacy program was the second project — the starting of a credit union. Briefly, a credit union is a cooperative bank designed to lend money at low rates of interest, to teach thrift and to develop a cooperative spirit in the community. Credit unions help the community by raising the buying power of the average family. A common bond must unite credit union members, such as membership in the same parish.

During the holidays three Class Four sodalists attended a seminar on credit unions. When these boys returned to school in September, they discussed the possibility of starting a credit union with a number of farmers in one of the more advanced literacy courses. These farmers were very agreeable to the idea and thirty of them decided to study the credit union idea. These study sessions lasted all through September, October, and part of November. By the end of November, the group was ready to write their by-laws. The by-laws were held up by the Department of Cooperatives because at that time credit unions were not very acceptable. The situation has changed, however, since independence. Eventually, the membership in this credit union was estimated to reach 150 farmers. In several of the other villages, the farmers are hoping to find out about the credit union idea and it is hoped to organize eventually the farmers in the neighboring areas.

By the end of the year, the Form One sodality group began to devise and work on the third socio-economic project. The whole school had been affected to a certain extent by what the Form Four sodality group had done, especially in the area of adult literacy. Many students were beginning to understand that in some way their life must be related to the masses and that their vocation calls for them to *serve* the masses. The Form One group had started to discuss a project dealing with agriculture. It would be the operation of a small experimental farm of one or two acres on part of the school compound that was not being used at the time.

This was a realistic project since the majority of people were engaged in agriculture, using rather primitive methods. Two problems needed to be overcome before this project could ever get on its feet. First, some way would have had to be found in order to get the farmers to participate in the project, and secondly, the group would have required the services of an expert technician connected with the Ministry of Agriculture. Neither one of these obstacles could have hindered or stopped the project but the second element was more difficult to overcome. It is not easy to find the right kind of agricultural technician. In Africa we need agricultural schools less than the advice of a highly-trained agriculturist who is sympathetic to the local culture and to self-help programs. This is not so easy to find as it sounds. Too many of the technicians are not prepared to work for and with the poor peasants, with humility and a spirit of service and sacrifice.

The Form Four group had in mind that the experimental agricultural farm would be the base for agricultural extension work. On this farm a small number of farmers would work in their traditional fashion, digging the soil with sticks. The students as the technicians would join these men as they worked and would show them little practices that might eventually lead to a different type of agriculture. This practical field method disturbs these people the least as the students tried to introduce changes.

In all of this work of using the school and the students to stimulate socio-economic progress in the rural community there is one important factor: the people must want the projects and they must supply the enterprise and the initiative. The tribe around this area is anxious for change, for improvement of their economic condition, for modern ideas and ways of doing things, and are just waiting for someone to stimulate them with new ideas.

The Apostolate in the Urban Community

To a great extent the Church has neglected the apostolate in the urban centers of Africa in favor of work in the rural areas. This is a serious mistake, for after all the great world mission of the Church was established for all time in the great urban centers of the ancient world. Athens, Corinth, Jerusalem, Alexandria, Rome — all these great urban centers of the ancient world were planted with the seeds of early Christianity and the Church's mission radiated out from these centers. Christianity came forth from the cities among the lower middle-class population whose spiritual need is the greatest and who listen most eagerly to the Word of God. So too in the modern world in the developing countries, the Church must once again concentrate her effort in the urban centers. She has not done this so far; she has concentrated far too much of her resources in the rural areas. It is in the direction of the poor peasants and workers of the cities that the main effort of the Church should be directed in the developing countries of Africa and Asia.

Because of the complexity of city life, it is much more difficult to discover what exactly is the role of the school in the urban community. We know quite easily the needs of the rural communities: adult education, credit unions, cooperatives, adaptation of modern agricultural methods and the introduction of small industries. The socioeconomic development of the city includes almost none of these. The community in most African cities already possess a smattering of education since it is the younger elements of African society who have migrated to the cities. If they do want adult literacy classes, then the Ministry of Education supplies evening continuation classes.

Credit unions and cooperatives are even more difficult to organize. City people have just developed a sense of belonging to a community; too many of them still find their security and sense of belonging back in some rural, tribal community. Very little family life exists since the wife is very often back in some village, cultivating three or four acres of land. She may have a few of the younger children with her while the older ones may be with their father who is working with the railways or an industry in the city. Such unstable conditions in the city make it almost impossible for such an organization as a credit union or a cooperative to develop.

The rural community emphasized the economic aspect of life; the city community was taken up with the social problems of life — lack of family life, poor living conditions, lack of recreational facilities, high rents, etc. The school in this second case tried to face all these issues. Both of these cases, incidentally, are from Kenya.

Quite by accident the Y.C.S. group came upon a project at a local orphanage operated by the Sisters of Charity. Some of the Y.C.S. members had been invited out for a dance with the secondary girls. It was discovered that the sisters needed help in the construction of roads and paths around the property as well as aid in preparing a section of the property for a vegetable garden. The Y.C.S. group discussed this project over several meetings and it was decided that they would organize the students in the different classes of the school so that it was a school project rather than a Y.C.S. project.

There remained the task of getting the students to participate. Forms One and Two presented no special problems since all the boys in the two Y.C.S. groups came from these Forms. As there were no Y.C.S. members among Form Three students, one member of the Second Form Y.C.S. group enlisted the support of two Form Three students who agreed to get the cooperation of the students in Form Three. About two weeks before the end of the second school term, a Y.C.S. member gave a talk in each class in the first three Forms; he explained the project and noted that he would return the next day in order to obtain the names of those students interested in the project. The senior form in the school, Form Four, was left out of the project completely, since they would be preparing for the Cambridge Examinations.

The Y.C.S. group collected over 100 names for this project. Much more could be said about this, but it suffices to note that a large number of students — around twenty on an average day — were drawn into this project.

This project has opened up to the Y.C.S. groups vast opportunities of participation in social development projects. First, each student in the senior Form devotes one afternoon a week to some social project. This may be voluntary work at one of the orphanages in the city, or it may be working at one of the many community centers, or working with the Social Service League. Secondly, during one vacation period in the year, the first three Forms in the school participate in voluntary self-help projects at the girls' orphanage. Thirdly, the Y.C.S. organized a study day for students from the secondary schools on city problems and on the vocation to serve the urban apostolate. Fourthly, the Y.C.S. groups would like to bring to the attention of other students the many needs for well-trained people to cope with city problems. The fields of architecture, engineering, city planning, child welfare work, and city government are particularly important in shaping the future destiny of African cities. Fifthly, the Y.C.S. groups are beginning to see that they must bring to the attention of the students the crisis that is going on before their eyes; social life here is poisoned by the disorganization of family life owing to the movement between the rural and urban areas and the lack of citizen responsibility for the welfare of the community. It has yet to be decided by the Y.C.S. groups how the students can be made conscious of these problems in urban life and their responsibility to do something about them. Perhaps the solution to make the students aware of city problems is to conduct study days and seminars for them devoted to analyzing city affairs. In any case, it is indeed the responsibility of our Y.C.S. groups to evolve an exposition of the social teachings of the Church with respect to our explosive developing city life.

The fruit of this entire program by the Y.C.S. should mean a revival of a concept and practice of civic virtue in a Christian sense. The fruit of such a renewed spirit of Christian civic enlightenment will be harvested in a program of urban social action aimed at creating a new society in a new city.

In Africa today it is not the mission of the Church to present an aggressive, proselytizing attitude, but rather it is her mission to orientate the new Africa in this difficult time of social upheavals and the expansion of scientific and industrial civilization. We should not be concerned with individual conversion primarily but rather with making our students socially conscious so that they will give a greater witness to Christ in the world and in society. This will all come about if we are really training our students to a greater social consciousness and if we are training them to a constant living of social charity and social justice. These students, if we train them properly, will hold a serious dialogue with the world; they will be the ones personally concerned with the salvation of their brothers, with making them living, human members of the People of God.

PART III

APPENDICES

Appendix A

SOME NATIONAL RESOURCE ORGANIZATIONS

Communications:

Columbia Broadcasting System (CBS) 485 Madison Avenue	New York, N. Y. 10022
National Broadcasting Corp. (NBC) Rockefeller Plaza	New York, N. Y. 10020
American Broadcasting Co. (ABC) 30 Rockefeller Plaza	New York, N. Y. 10020
American Federation of Arts 41 East 65th Street	New York, N. Y. 10021
The Advertising Council 25 West 45th Street	New York, N. Y. 10036
1200 Eighteenth Street, N.W.	Washington, D.C. 20006
American Association of Advertising Agencies 200 Park Avenue	New York, N. Y. 10017
National Catholic Center for Radio, Television, Film and Press 830 Bathurst Street	Toronto 4, Ont., Canada
National Audience Board, Inc. 152 East End Avenue	New York, N. Y. 10028
National Office for Decent Literature (NODL) 33 East Congress Parkway	Chicago, Ill. 60605
National Legion of Decency 453 Madison Avenue	New York, N. Y. 10022
Catholic Broadcasters Association University of Detroit 4001 West McNicholas Road	Detroit, Mich. 48221

American Federation of Film Societies
1209 West Jarvis Avenue   Chicago, Ill. 60626

Federation of Motion Picture Councils
17 Summit Street   East Orange, N. J. 07017

Business, Labor, and Economic Organizations:

Chamber of Commerce of the
  United States
1615 H. Street, N.W.   Washington, D.C. 20006

Foundation for Economic Education
  (FEE)
30 South Broadway   Irvington-on-Hudson,
                                            N. Y. 10533

Association of Better Business
  Bureaus, Inc.
723 Chrysler Building   New York, N. Y. 10017

Committee for Economic Development
  (CED)
711 Fifth Avenue   New York, N. Y. 10022

American Federation of Labor —
  Congress of Industrial Organizations
  (AFL-CIO)
815 Sixteenth Street, N.W.   Washington, D.C. 20006

National Association of Manufacturers
  (NAM)
918 Sixteenth Street, N.W.   Washington, D.C. 20006

National Industrial Conference Board
845 Third Avenue   New York, N. Y. 10022

National Management Association
333 West First Street   Dayton, Ohio 45402

Religious Organizations — Catholic:

U. S. Catholic Conference, Inc.
1312 Massachusetts Avenue, N.W.   Washington, D.C. 20005

Education, Press, Legal, Lay Organizations, Social Action, Youth, and Immigration Departments. Also offices of the National Council of Catholic Men (NCCM), National Council of Catholic Women (NCCW), Confraternity of Christian Doctrine

(CCD), National Newman Apostolate, National Catholic Coordinating Committee on Economic Opportunity, National Federation of Sodalities. Serves as secretariat for the National Conference of Catholic Bishops.

National Catholic Laymen's Retreat Conference P. O. Box 222	Covington, Ky. 41018
Liturgical Conference 2900 Newton Street, N.E.	Washington, D.C. 20018
Conference of Major Religious Superiors of Women's Institutes 2158 Florida Avenue, N.W.	Washington, D.C. 20008
Association for International Development (AID) 374 Grand Street	Paterson, N. J. 07505
Catholic Students' Mission Crusade (CSMC) 5100 Shattuck Avenue	Cincinnati, Ohio 45226
Christian Family Movement (CFM) 1655 West Jackson Boulevard	Chicago, Ill. 60612
Columbian Squires P. O. Drawer 1670	New Haven, Conn. 06507
Bureau of Catholic Indian Missions 2021 H Street, N.W.	Washington, D.C. 20006
Extension Lay Volunteers 1307 South Wabash Avenue	Chicago, Ill. 60605
Front Line University of Dayton	Dayton, Ohio 45409
Foundation for International Cooperation (FIC) 207 East 37th Street	New York, N. Y. 10016
The Gabriel Richard Institute 305 Michigan Avenue	Detroit, Mich. 48226
The Grail Movement Grailville	Loveland, Ohio 45140
Better World Movement 329 Victoria Road	Asheville, N. C. 28801

Papal Volunteers for Latin America
(PAVLA)
22 West Monroe Street   Chicago, Ill. 60603

United Missionary Air Transport and
Training (UMATT)
University of Dayton   Dayton, Ohio 45409

Serra International
22 West Monroe Street   Chicago, Ill. 60603

Young Christian Workers (YCW)
1655 Jackson Boulevard   Chicago, Ill. 60612

Young Christian Students (YCS)
1655 West Jackson   Chicago, Ill. 60612

The Christophers
18 East 48th Street   New York, N. Y. 10017

Holy Name Society
141 East 65th Street   New York, N. Y. 10002

Conference of Major Religious
Superiors of Men's Institutes
1312 Massachusetts Avenue, N.W.   Washington, D.C. 20005

Pontifical Society for the Propagation
of the Faith
366 Fifth Avenue   New York, N. Y. 10001

St. Vincent DePaul Society
2041 Railway Exchange Building   St. Louis, Missouri 63101

Knights of Columbus (K of C)
Columbus Plaza   New Haven, Conn. 06507

Pax Romana
1701 Fribourg, Switzerland
United Nations Office:
207 East 37th Street   New York, N. Y.

Center for Applied Research in the
Apostolate (CARA)
1717 Massachusetts Avenue, N.W.   Washington, D.C. 20036

Catholic Inter-American Cooperation
Conference (CICOP)
410 Brady Street   Davenport, Iowa 52801

Catholic Church Extension Society
1307 South Wabash Avenue   Chicago, Ill. 60605

Catholic Hospital Association 1438 South Grand Boulevard	St. Louis, Missouri 63104
St. Paul's Guild 31 East 50th Street	New York, N. Y. 10022
Catholic Central Union (Verein) 3835 Westminster Place	St. Louis, Missouri 63108

Religious Organizations — Protestant:

Salvation Army 120-130 W. Fourteenth Street	New York, N. Y. 10011
Volunteers of America 340 West 85th Street	New York, N. Y. 10024
National Council of Churches 475 Riverside Drive	New York, N. Y. 10027
Young Men's Christian Association (YMCA) 291 Broadway	New York, N. Y. 10007
Young Women's Christian Association (YWCA) 600 Lexington Avenue	New York, N. Y. 10022
American Friends Service Committee 160 North Fifteenth Street	Philadelphia, Penn. 19102
American Council of Christian Churches Room 1729 15 Park Row	New York, N. Y. 10038
U. S. Conference, World Council of Churches 156 Fifth Avenue	New York, N. Y. 10010
American Association of Theological Schools 1250 Knott Building	Dayton, Ohio 45402
Americans United for Separation of Church and State 1683 Massachusetts Avenue, N.W.	Washington, D.C. 20006
Lutheran Laymen's League 2185 Hampton Avenue	St. Louis, Missouri 63110

Youth for Christ (YFC)
1 N 310 Main Street — Wheaton, Ill. 60187

Religious Organizations — Jewish:
Central Conference of American
   Rabbis
40 West 68th Street — New York, N. Y. 10023

American Jewish Committee
165 East 56th Street — New York, N. Y. 10022

American Jewish Congress
15 East 84th Street — New York, N. Y. 10028

B'nai B'rith
1640 Rhode Island Avenue, N.W. — Washington, D.C. 20006

National Jewish Welfare Board
145 East 32nd Street — New York, N. Y. 10016

American Zionist Council
342 Madison Avenue — New York, N. Y. 10017

Hadassah
65 East 52nd Street — New York, N. Y. 10022

Religious Organizations — Other:
National Conference of Christians and
   Jews (NCCJ)
43 West 57th Street — New York, N. Y. 10019

American Humanist Association
Springfield Pike — Yellow Springs, Ohio
   45387

Moral Re-Armanent (MRA)
Cedar Point — Mackinac Island,
   Mich. 49757

Unitarian Universalist Fellowship
   for Social Justice
245 Second Street, N.E. — Washington, D.C. 20002

Civic Clubs:
Elks
2750 Lake View Avenue — Chicago, Ill. 60614

National League of Masonic Clubs
(Masons)
6 North Avenue, West   Cranford, N. J. 07016

Kiwanis International
520 North Michigan Avenue   Chicago, Ill. 60611

Lions Clubs
209 North Michigan Avenue   Chicago, Ill. 60601

Optimists International
1721 Railway Exchange Building   St. Louis, Missouri 63101

Rotary International
1600 Ridge Avenue   Evanston, Ill. 60201

Educational and Professional Organizations:

American Council of Learned Societies
345 East 46th Street   New York, N. Y. 10017

College Theology Society
Dunbarton College of the Holy Cross   Washington, D.C. 20008

American Bar Association (ABA)
1155 East 60th Street   Chicago, Ill. 60637

American Medical Association (AMA)
535 North Dearborn Street   Chicago, Ill. 60610

American Library Association (ALA)
50 East Huron Street   Chicago, Ill. 60611

Catholic Library Association
461 West Lancaster Avenue   Haverford, Penn. 19041

American Personnel and Guidance
Association
1534 "O" Street, N.W.   Washington, D.C. 20005

National Educational Association
(NEA)
1201 Sixteenth Street, N.W.   Washington, D.C. 20006

Also offices for American Association of School Administrators
(AASA), National Association of Secondary School Principals
(NASSP), National Council of Teachers of Mathematics,
National Science Teachers Association, National Council for
the Social Studies, National Business Education Association,
National Training Laboratories, American Association of
Physics Teachers, National Association of Student Councils.

Educational Services, Inc.
164 Main Street   Watertown, Mass. 02172

Great Books Foundation
37 South Wabash   Chicago, Ill. 60603

Council for Basic Education
725 Fifteenth Street, N.W.   Washington, D.C. 20005

National Association of University
    Professors (AAUP)
1785 Massachusetts Avenue, N.W.   Washington, D.C. 20036

Citizens for Educational Freedom
3109 South Grand Boulevard   St. Louis, Missouri 63118

Fund for the Advancement of
    Education
477 Madison Avenue   New York, N. Y. 10022

American Council on Education (ACE)
1785 Massachusetts Avenue, N.W.   Washington, D.C. 20036

National School Boards Association
1940 Sheridan Road   Evanston, Ill. 60201

National Catholic Educational
    Association
1785 Massachusetts Avenue, N.W.   Washington, D.C. 20036

Religious Education Association
545 West 111th Street   New York, N. Y. 10025

National Catholic Guidance
    Conference
2401 69th Street   Kenosha, Wis. 53140

United States National Student
    Association
3457 Chestnut Street   Philadelphia, Penn.
                                            19104

Welfare Organizations:

American Public Welfare Association
1313 East Sixtieth Street   Chicago, Ill. 60637

Alcoholics Anonymous (AA)
P. O. Box 459   Grand Central Annex,
                                            N. Y.

Big Brothers of America
1007 Suburban Station Building   Philadelphia, Penn.
                                            19103

National Council on Family Relations
1219 University Avenue, S.E.   Minneapolis, Minn.
                                            55414

American Council to Improve Our
   Neighborhoods (ACTION)
2 West 46th Street   New York, N. Y. 10036

National Confederation of American
   Ethnic Groups
1761 R Street, N.W.   Washington, D.C. 20009

Planned Parenthood Federation of
   America
501 Madison Avenue   New York, N. Y. 10022

National Association for Retarded
   Children
99 University Place   New York, N. Y. 10003

National Federation of Settlements
226 West 47th Street   New York, N. Y. 10036

National Council of Senior Citizens
1627 K Street, N.W.   Washington, D.C. 20006

Al-Anon Family Group Headquarters
125 East 23rd Street   New York, N. Y. 10010

Boys' Clubs of America
771 First Avenue   New York, N. Y. 10017

Community Service
114 East Whiteman Street   Yellow Springs, Ohio
                                            45387

Civil Rights Groups:
American Civil Liberties Association
   (ACLU)
170 Fifth Avenue   New York, N. Y. 10011

National Committee Against
   Discrimination in Housing
323 Lexington Avenue   New York, N. Y. 10016

National Conference on Religion
  and Race
Room 632
150 Fifth Avenue   New York, N. Y. 10011

National Urban League
14 East 48th Street   New York, N. Y. 10017

Anti-Defamation League of B'nai B'rith
515 Madison Avenue   New York, N. Y. 10022

National Association for the
  Advancement of Colored People
  (NAACP)
20 West 40th Street   New York, N. Y. 10018

Student Non-Violent Coordinating
  Committee (SNICK)
6 Raymond Street, N.W.   Atlanta, Georgia 30314

Congress of Racial Equality (CORE)
38 Park Row   New York, N. Y. 10038

National Catholic Conference for
  Interracial Justice (NCCIJ)
1307 South Wabash Avenue   Chicago, Ill. 60610

Leadership Conference on Civil Rights
20 West 40th Street   New York, N. Y. 10018

National Council of Negro Women
1318 Vermont Avenue, N.W.   Washington, D.C. 20005

Southern Christian Leadership
  Conference (SCLC)
334 Auburn Avenue, N.E.   Atlanta, Georgia 30303

Political and Government Organizations:

Democratic National Committee
1730 "K" Street, N.W.   Washington, D.C. 20006

Republican National Committee
1625 Eye Street, N.W.   Washington, D.C. 20006

Americans for Democratic Action
  (ADA)
1341 Connecticut Avenue, N.W.   Washington, D.C. 20006

John Birch Society
395 Concord Street   Belmont, Mass. 02178

International City Managers
  Association (IMCA)
1313 East Sixtieth Street   Chicago, Ill. 60637

American Society for Public
  Administration (ASPA)
1329 Eighteenth Street, N.W.   Washington, D.C. 20036

League of Women Voters of the
  United States
1026 Seventeenth Street, N.W.   Washington, D.C. 20036

International Association of Chiefs
  of Police (IACP)
1319 Eighteenth Street, N.W.   Washington, D.C. 20036

Conservative Clubs of America
2020 West Montrose Avenue   Chicago, Ill. 60618

An exhaustive list of groups is provided in the *Encyclopedia of Associations* (Gale Research Company, 1964, 4th Edition). Over 12,500 groups are listed and briefly described.

Appendix B

TECHNIQUE FOR A PROBLEM CENSUS

The type of problem census illustrated here can be undertaken as a class project to learn of the composition of the school student body, or as a community or neighborhood survey. In any case, participants should be assured of anonymity so that their answers are more likely to be frank. It should be understood that the census may not reveal real problems so much as it will reveal what people *think* are the community's problems. The questions used in this survey here have been gathered from a number of different questionnaires. Depending upon particular interests, the questions can be varied, added to, or deleted, but this illustration will show the teacher what type of information may be of value. This material is based on a series of questionnaires used in several central Missouri cities.

Typical Community Problems that May be Encountered
Economic
     poverty
     unemployment
     waste of natural resources
     slum conditions
Cultural
     apathy
     cultural deprivation
     irreligion
     school drop-outs and underachievement
     irreligion

Social
> family breakdown — divorce, desertion, separation
> illegitimacy
> discrimination in housing, employment, education
> drug addiction
> delinquency and crime
> sexual perversion
> neighborhood deterioration

Health
> mental illness
> disease
> alcoholism

Failure of Public Agencies
> poor schools, overcrowding, lack of facilities
> lack of support of voluntary agencies
> inadequate tax structures
> lack of cooperation among different area governments
> poor sanitary conditions — sewers, garbage collection, street cleaning
> lack of recreation and park facilities
> zoning and housing violations
> poor street repair and poor street lighting

In taking a community or neighborhood survey, the teacher may wish to reflect upon the moral and religious implications of what is revealed, on what can be done to remedy the situations described, or on what the role of the school can be in the community. The school and the faculty may simply want background information. This questionnaire is divided into three areas: what needs to be accomplished and who can accomplish it, what residents think of available services, and what the character of the residents answering the survey questions is.

A Community Survey
1. What one thing accomplished in this community in the past five years has made the greatest contribution to this

community?
2. Whom do you believe was most responsible for accomplishing this improvement? Individuals? Groups?
3. What do you think are some of the most pressing problems in our community at this time?
4. What one single improvement would you suggest that the community make in the next five years?
5. If you were to push for the adoption of the idea you mentioned in Question #4, to whom would you turn for help in putting over the project? Individuals? Groups?
6. Whom do you think would be against your proposal? Individuals? Groups?
7. In your neighborhood, who is active in getting things done?
8. Which of the neighborhood leaders you mentioned in Question #7 do you believe becomes most involved in city-wide projects?
9. Are most of your family purchases made in this neighborhood?
10. Where do you go for items you do not purchase in the neighborhood?
11. What items do you most often buy outside the neighborhood?

> groceries   hardware
> appliances   clothing
> furniture   drugs
> other (please list)

12. Do you think that the neighborhood business district appearance and upkeep is satisfactory?
13. Do you have a bank account in the neighborhood?
14. How do you rate existing recreational facilities serving the following age groups in the neighborhood?

>   *adequate   inadequate   no opinion*
> children
> teenagers
> young adults
> middle aged

senior citizens
15. What, if any, recreational facilities would you like to see added?
16. What services can the church offer to develop more interest in church life in the neighborhood?
17. Have you children in the public schools? In parochial schools?
18. What curriculum or subject offerings would you like to see in the schools?
19. List what you regard as strong points and weak points of our public schools. Parochial schools.
20. Rate the following public services:

	adequate	*inadequate*	*no opinion*
police protection			
fire protection			
streets			
street lighting			
water service			
electricity			
telephone			
parking facilities			
public library			
garbage collection			
recreation			
parks			

21. Rate the following community services:

	adequate	*inadequate*	*no opinion*
hospitals			
nursing homes			
public health services			
doctors			
dentists			
nurses			

22. With what organizations in the community are you affiliated?

	member	*active*
Rotary		
Kiwanis		

Chamber of Commerce
Veterans of Foreign Wars
American Legion
Knights of Columbus
Parent-Teachers Association
(Others that are locally active may be listed.)

23. Are you a church member?

	member	attend regularly	active in church groups
Assembly of God			
Baptist			
Catholic			
Christian			
Church of God (Holiness)			
Episcopal			
Evangelical and Reformed			
Jewish			
Lutheran			
Methodist			
Presbyterian			
Other (please list)			

24. Indicate the category or categories that best describe your family's source of income.

category	all	most	some
salaried			
business			
farm			
pension			
other (please list)			

25. Which best describes your family's income last year?

less than $3000	$ 7000 — 9000
$3000 — 5000	$ 9000 — 11,000
$5000 — 7000	$11,000 and over

26. How many years have you lived in this neighborhood?

27. How many members of your household are in each of the following age groups?

1 — 6	20 — 24	41 — 45	61 — 65
7 — 12	25 — 30	46 — 50	65 — 70
13 — 15	31 — 35	51 — 55	70 — 75
16 — 19	36 — 40	56 — 60	over 75

28. What is the highest grade finished in school by the head of the house? (Can be varied to include all adult members.)

29. Please indicate sex.   Marital status.   Race.

If the surveyor has some definite points on which he seeks the opinion of the community or the neighborhood, a useful variety of question is the "agree — don't agree" type. These questions can ask for opinions on community services:

> Springfield should have an airport.
> Verona schools should have adult education courses.

They may also reflect attitudes:

> A few people control what happens in Canoga Park.
> There are rivalries between Blacksburg and other neighboring small towns.
> Most people in Valdosta are friendly toward newcomers.

This type of question has the advantage of being quickly answered, even when the questionnaire is long. It has the disadvantage of being difficult to construct in order to avoid leading questions. The respondents are asked to check off "agree," "don't agree," or "no opinion" for each statement.

The average community survey will run from five to ten pages in printed or mimeographed form. This is long for many people, but size, as well as types of questions, can be adjusted for particular interests. And, as many teachers will notice immediately, there are situations in which some questions are inappropriate or too personal.

Appendix C

SUGGESTED READINGS

Adrian, Charles R. (editor), *Social Science and Community Action* (Michigan State University Press, 1960)

Banfield, Edward C., *Political Influence* (Free Press, 1961)

Banfield, Edward C., and Morton Grodzins, *Government and Housing in Metropolitan Areas* (McGraw-Hill, 1958)

Banfield, Edward C., and James Q. Wilson, *City Politics* (Harvard University Press, 1963)

Bendix, Reinhard, and Seymour M. Lipset, *Class, Status and Power* (Free Press, 1957)

Bollens, John C., (editor), *Exploring the Metropolitan Community* (University of California Press, 1961)

Bollens, John C., and Henry J. Schmandt, *The Metropolis* (Harper and Row, 1965)

Coleman, James S., *Community Conflict* (Free Press, 1956)

Conant, James B., *Slums and Suburbs* (McGraw-Hill, 1961)

Connery, Robert H., and Richard H. Leach, *The Federal Government and Metropolitan Areas* (Harvard University Press, 1960)

Cox, Harvey, *The Secular City* (Macmillan, 1965)

Dahl, Robert, *Who Governs?* (Yale University Press, 1961)

Dobriner, William M., *The Suburban Community* (Putnam, 1958)

Duhl, Leonard J., (editor), *The Urban Condition: People and Policy in the Metropolis* (Basic Books, 1963)

Elias, C. E., Jr., James Gillies, and Svend Riemer (editors), *Metropolis: Values in Conflict* (Wadsworth, 1964)

Gans, Herbert, *The Urban Villagers* (Free Press, 1962)

Glazer, Nathan, and Daniel P. Moynihan, *Beyond the Melting Pot* (Massachusetts Institute of Technology, 1963)

Gottman, Jean, *Megalopolis* (Twentieth Century Fund, 1961)

Greer, Scott, *The Emerging City* (Free Press, 1962)

Greer, Scott, *Governing the Metropolis* (John Wiley, 1962)

Greer, Scott, *Metropolitics* (Wiley, 1962)

Harrington, Michael, *The Other America: Poverty in the United States* (Macmillan, 1962)

Hunter, Floyd, *Community Power Structure* (Doubleday Anchor Books, 1963)

Intercultural Relations Department, Detroit Public Schools, *The 4th "R"* (Detroit Public Schools, 1965)

Kaplan, Harold, *Urban Renewal Politics* (Columbia University Press, 1963)

King, Martin L., *Why We Can't Wait* (Signet Books, 1961)

Lee, Eugene C., *The Politics of Nonpartisanship* (University of California Press, 1960)

Lowry, Ritchie P., *Who's Running This Town?* (Harper and Row, 1965)

Martin, Roscoe C., *The Cities and the Federal System* (Atherton Press, 1965)

McAvoy, Thomas, C.S.C., *Roman Catholicism and the American Way of Life* (Notre Dame University Press, 1960)

Meyerson, Martin, Barbara Terrett, and William L. C. Wheaton, *Housing, People and Cities* (McGraw-Hill, 1962)

Mumford, Lewis, *The City in History* (Harcourt, Brace and World, 1961)

New City

Polsby, Nelson, *Community Power and Political Theory* (Yale University Press, 1963)

Presthus, Robert V., *Men at the Top* (Oxford University Press, 1964)

Riessman, Frank, *The Culturally Deprived Child* (Harper and Row, 1962)

Rodwin, Lloyd, *The Future Metropolis* (George Braziller, 1961)

Scientific American, Vol. 213, No. 3, (September, 1965)

Swanson, Bert E., *The Struggle for Equality* (Dobbs, Dorman, 1966)

United States Department of Health, Education, and Welfare; Office of Education, *Programs for the Educationally Disadvantaged,* U. S. Office of Education Bulletin 1963, #17

Urban Affairs Quarterly

Weaver, Robert C., *The Urban Complex: Human Values in Urban Life* (Doubleday, 1964)

Weber, Max, *The City* (Free Press, 1958)